# 101 C
# Programming
# Challenges

**First Edition**

**Yashavant Kanetkar**
**Aditya Kanetkar**

**FIRST EDITION 2017**

Copyright © BPB Publications, INDIA
ISBN :978-93-8655-142-9

**Distributors:**

**BPB PUBLICATIONS** 20,
Ansari Road, Darya Ganj
New Delhi-110002
Ph: 23254990/23254991

**BPB BOOK CENTRE**
376 Old Lajpat Rai Market,
Delhi-110006
Ph: 23861747

**COMPUTER BOOK CENTRE**
12, Shrungar Shopping Centre,
M.G.Road, BENGALURU–560001
Ph: 25587923/25584641

**DECCAN AGENCIES**
4-3-329, Bank Street,
Hyderabad-500195
Ph: 24756967/24756400

**MICRO MEDIA**
Shop No. 5, Mahendra Chambers, 150 DN
Rd. Next to Capital Cinema, V.T. (C.S.T.)
Station, MUMBAI-400 001 Ph:
22078296/22078297

Published by Manish Jain for BPB Publications, 20, Ansari Road, Darya Ganj, New Delhi-110002 and Printed him at Repro India Pvt Ltd, Mumbai

*We know that you are here with us*
*on this day...*

## About Yashavant Kanetkar

Through his books and Quest Courseware DVDs on C, C++, Java, .NET, Embedded Systems, etc. Yashavant Kanetkar has created, moulded and groomed lacs of IT careers in the last two decades. Yashavant's books and Quest DVDs have made a significant contribution in creating top-notch IT manpower in India and abroad.

Yashavant's books are globally recognized and millions of students / professionals have benefitted from them. Yashavant's books have been translated into Hindi, Gujarati, Japanese, Korean and Chinese languages. Many of his books are published in India, USA, Japan, Singapore, Korea and China.

Yashavant is a much sought after speaker in the IT field and has conducted seminars/workshops at TedEx, IITs, RECs and global software companies.

Yashavant has recently been honored with the prestigious "Distinguished Alumnus Award" by IIT Kanpur for his entrepreneurial, professional and academic excellence. This award was given to top 50 alumni of IIT Kanpur who have made significant contribution towards their profession and betterment of society in the last 50 years.

In recognition of his immense contribution to IT education in India, he has been awarded the "Best .NET Technical Contributor" and "Most Valuable Professional" awards by Microsoft for 5 successive years.

Yashavant holds a BE from VJTI Mumbai and M.Tech. from IIT Kanpur.

## About Aditya Kanetkar

 Aditya Kanetkar holds a Master's Degree in Computer Science from Georgia Tech, Atlanta. Prior to that, he completed his Bachelor's Degree in Computer Science and Engineering from IIT Guwahati. He is currently working as a Software Engineer at Oracle America Inc. at Redwood City, California.

Aditya is a very keen programmer since his intern days at Redfin, Amazon Inc. and Arista Networks. His current passion is anything remotely connected to Java Technologies, Android programming and Databases.

# Preface

Belief is one thing, facts might be different! Today, in most of the higher secondary boards in the country, C language is taught in XI$^{th}$ standard and C++ in XII$^{th}$ standard. This results into a very common outcome—the student is neither good at C, nor at C++. Instead of getting to know the nuances of C language, he ends up merely scratching the surface. Same is the story of C++. So when he enters an Engineering college or a Science college he is low on confidence, having hardly spent any time with either of the languages. In college also, he meets the same fate. In one semester some parts of C programming are taught and in the next semester some parts of C++ programming are taught.

In further semesters he is required to build data structures, complete programming assignments in other subjects, or implement mini-projects or a major project in C, C++ or Java. Problem is, his fundamentals are so weak that after making some progress he hits a wall. That's when the feeling starts sinking that he migrated to newer languages too early, without giving enough time to have a rock solid foundation in C programming.

Unfortunately, there are hardly any C programming books which go beyond the most rudimentary C programs and test the knowledge and competence of the reader in C programming.

We hope that this book would fill that void. Not only have we put together 101 Challenges in C programming, we have also organized them according to features of C programming one needs to use to solve them. If you are not able to solve a challenge or need a hint to solve it, there are ready-made solutions to each of the 101 challenges. In addition, the book also shows sample runs of these solutions, so that you get to know what input to give and what output to expect while solving a challenge. Each challenge is also followed up by a crisp explanation about the vital issues in the program solution. We hope you would find this aspect of the book—of putting everything about a challenge together—quite useful. We have also used illustrative icons to highlight the Challenge, Solution, Sample Run and Explanation so that you have no difficulty in spotting them.

So using this book not only would you be able to hone your programming skills, but also become a more mature C programmer.

We urge you to solve all the challenges in the book before migrating to learning C++ or Java. If you do so you would be on much surer grounds while learning the newer languages.

All the best and happy programming!

**Yashavant Kanetkar**

**Aditya Kanetkar**

# CHALLENGES

*Index it* (Challenge 11)
*Index it* (Challenge 13)
*Index it* (Challenge 22)
*Index it* (Challenge 23)
*Index it* (Challenge 24)
*Index it* (Challenge 29)
*Index it* (Challenge 30)

# 01 / Total Challenges: 7

# Basic Control Flow Challenges

In a C program the sequence of execution of instructions is governed by the control instruction that is used. Unless explicitly mentioned, instructions in a C program are executed one after the other or sequentially. Challenges 1 to 7 in this chapter deal with programs that need sequence control instruction to implement their logic.

## Challenge 01

Write a program to round off an integer **i** to the next largest multiple of another integer **j**. For example, 256 days when rounded off to the next largest multiple divisible by a week results into 259.

## Solution

```c
#include <stdio.h>
int main( )
{
    int  i, j, k ;

    printf ( "Enter values of i and j:\n" ) ;
    scanf ( "%d %d", &i, &j ) ;

    k = i + j - i % j ;

    printf ( "Next largest multiple = %d\n", k ) ;
    return 0 ;
}
```

## Sample Run

After 25 days R = 7958 W = 1800
After 50 days R = 6654 W = 1602

## Explanation

Suppose value of **i** and **j** are entered as 256 and 7, then **k** evaluates to 259 which is the next largest multiple of 7 after 256.

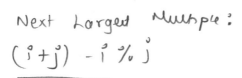

Next Largest Multiple:

$$( i + j ) - i \% j$$

## Challenge 02

Write a program to receive Cartesian coordinates (x, y) of a point and convert them into polar coordinates (r, φ).

## Solution

```c
/* Convert Cartesian coordinates to Polar coordinates */
# include <stdio.h>
# include <math.h>

int main( )
{
    float  x, y, r, theta ;

    printf ( "Enter x and y coordinates:\n " ) ;
    scanf ( "%f %f", &x, &y ) ;

    r = sqrt ( x * x + y * y ) ;
    theta = atan2 ( y, x ) ;
    theta = theta * 180 / 3.14 ;   /* convert to degrees */
    printf ( "r = %f theta = %f\n", r, theta ) ;

    return 0 ;
}
```

## Sample Run

```
Enter x and y coordinates:
12 12
r = 16.970562  theta = 44.981895
```

## Explanation

In Mathematics, a point in a plane can be represented using either Cartesian coordinate system or Polar coordinate system. Cartesian system specifies each point uniquely in a plane by a pair of numerical coordinates, (x, y). The Polar coordinate system specifies each point by a distance from origin and an angle from a reference direction.

Following formulae are used to convert a point in Cartesian coordinate system to Polar coordinate system.

$$r = \sqrt{x^2 + y^2}$$

$$\varphi = \tan^{-1}(y/x)$$

Note that to compute tan inverse we are using the function **atan2( )** rather than **atan( )**. This is because **atan( )** returns value of angle in only in 1st and 4th quadrant, whereas **atan2( )** returns value from 1st, 2nd, 3rd or 4th quadrant appropriately.

## Challenge  03

Two numbers are input through the keyboard into two locations **x** and **y**. Write a program to interchange the contents of **x** and **y.**

Swap

## Solution

```
/* Method: I */
/* Interchanging contents of two variables x & y */
# include <stdio.h>
int main( )
{
    int  x, y, t ;

    printf ( "Enter the number at location x:\n" ) ;
    scanf ( "%d", &x ) ;
    printf ( "Enter the number at location y:\n" ) ;
    scanf ( "%d", &y ) ;

    /* Interchange contents of x and y using t as temporary variable */
    t = x ;
    x = y ;
    y = t ;

    printf ( "Number at location x = %d\n", x ) ;
    printf ( "Number at location y = %d\n", y ) ;
```

```
        return 0 ;
}

/* Method: II */
/* Interchanging contents of two variables x & y */

#include <stdio.h>
int main( )
{
    int  x, y ;

        printf ( "Enter the number at location x: \n" ) ;
        scanf ( "%d", &x ) ;
        printf ( "Enter the number at location y: \n" ) ;
        scanf ( "%d", &y ) ;

        x = x + y ;
        y = x - y ;
        x = x - y ;

        printf ( "Number at location x: %d\n", x ) ;
        printf ( "Number at location y: %d\n", y ) ;

        return 0 ;
}
```

$i = 2, \quad j = 3$

$$i = i + j \quad = \quad 5 = 2 + 3$$
$$j = i - j \quad = \quad 2 = 5 - 3$$
$$i = i - j \quad = \quad 3 = 5 - 2$$

## Sample Run

```
Enter the number at location x:
50
Enter the number at location y:
100
Number at location x: 100
Number at location y: 50
```

## Explanation

Interchanging contents of two variables can be done using two methods—using a third variable **t** or without using the third variable. Both methods are given in the programs above.

Note that the first method can be used for exchanging numbers, names, dates, etc. whereas the second method can be used only for exchanging numbers, as this method involves arithmetic operations which can be done only on numbers.

## Challenge  04

The weight of a commodity is input through the keyboard. Write a program to convert and print this weight in grams, quintals, metric tons and pounds.

## Solution

```c
/* Conversion of weight */
#include <stdio.h>
int main( )
{
    float  kg, g, qt, ton, lbs ;

    printf ( "Enter weight in kilograms: \n" ) ;
    scanf ( "%f", &kg ) ;

    g = kg * 1000.0 ;
    qt = kg / 100.0 ;
    ton = kg / 1000.0 ;
    lbs = kg * 2.204 ;

    printf ( "Equivalent weight in grams = %f\n", g ) ;
    printf ( "Equivalent weight in quintals = %f\n", qt ) ;
    printf ( "Equivalent weight in metric tonnes = %f\n", ton ) ;
    printf ( "Equivalent weight in pounds = %f\n", lbs ) ;

    return 0 ;
```

}

## Sample Run

Enter weight in kilograms:
45.87
Equivalent weight in grams: 45870.000000
Equivalent weight in quintals: 0.458700
Equivalent weight in metric tonnes: 0.045870
Equivalent weight in pounds: 101.097481

## Explanation

The program uses the following conversion formulae:

1 kg = 1000 gm
1 quintal = 100 kg
1 ton = 1000 kg
1 kg = 2.2024 lbs

 ## Challenge  05

Paper of size A0 has dimensions 1189 mm x 841 mm. Each subsequent size A(n) is defined as A(n-1) cut in half parallel to its shorter sides. Write a program to calculate and print paper sizes A0, A1, A2, ... A8.

## Solution

```c
/* Calculation of PaperSizes A0 to A8 */
# include <stdio.h>

int main( )
{
    int  a0ht, a0wd ;
    int  a1ht, a1wd, a2ht, a2wd ;
    int  a3ht, a3wd, a4ht, a4wd ;
    int  a5ht, a5wd, a6ht, a6wd ;
    int  a7ht, a7wd, a8ht, a8wd ;
```

```
        a0ht = 1189 ;
        a0wd = 841 ;
        printf ( "Size of A0 paper Height = %d Width = %d\n", a0ht, a0wd ) ;

        a1ht = a0wd ;
        a1wd = a0ht / 2 ;
        printf ( "Size of A1 paper Height = %d Width = %d\n", a1ht, a1wd ) ;

        a2ht = a1wd ;
        a2wd = a1ht / 2 ;
        printf ( "Size of A2 paper Height = %d Width = %d\n", a2ht, a2wd ) ;

        a3ht = a2wd ;
        a3wd = a2ht / 2 ;
        printf ( "Size of A3 paper Height = %d Width = %d\n", a3ht, a3wd ) ;

        a4ht = a3wd ;
        a4wd = a3ht / 2 ;
        printf ( "Size of A4 paper Height = %d Width = %d\n", a4ht, a4wd ) ;

        a5ht = a4wd ;
        a5wd = a4ht / 2 ;
        printf ( "Size of A5 paper Height = %d Width = %d\n", a5ht, a5wd ) ;

        a6ht = a5wd ;
        a6wd = a5ht / 2 ;
        printf ( "Size of A6 paper Height = %d Width = %d\n", a6ht, a6wd ) ;

        a7ht = a6wd ;
        a7wd = a6ht / 2 ;
        printf ( "Size of A7 paper Height = %d Width = %d\n", a7ht, a7wd ) ;

        a8ht = a7wd ;
        a8wd = a7ht / 2 ;
        printf ( "Size of A8 paper Height = %d Width = %d\n", a8ht, a8wd ) ;

        return 0 ;
}
```

## Sample Run

Size of A0 Paper Height = 1189 Width = 841
Size of A1 Paper Height = 841 Width = 594
Size of A2 Paper Height = 594 Width = 420
Size of A3 Paper Height = 420 Width = 297
Size of A4 Paper Height = 297 Width = 210
Size of A5 Paper Height = 210 Width = 148
Size of A6 Paper Height = 148 Width = 105
Size of A7 Paper Height = 105 Width = 74
Size of A8 Paper Height = 74 Width = 52

## Explanation

The paper sizes like A0, A1, A2, etc. follow two rules:

(a)  The length to breadth ratio of each paper size is equal to 1.414.

(b)  As we proceed from A0 to A1 to A2, etc. the length of each subsequent paper size is equal to the width of the previous paper size and its width is equal to half the length of previous paper size. This is shown in Figure 1.1.

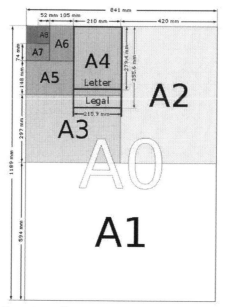

Figure 1.1. *Different paper sizes.*

The program uses rule (b) above to compute the length and breadth of each paper size.

## Challenge 06

Consider a currency system in which there are notes of seven denominations, namely, Re. 1, Rs. 2, Rs. 5, Rs. 10, Rs. 50, Rs. 100. If a sum of Rs. N is entered through the keyboard, write a program to compute the smallest number of notes that will combine to give Rs. N.

### Solution

```
/* Smallest number of notes that will combine to give the amount */
# include <stdio.h>
```

dollars

| | |
|---|---|
| 1 cent | 1 dollar |
| 5 cents | 20 dollar |
| 10 cents | 50 dollar |
| | 100 dollars. |

```
int main( )
{
    int  amt, nohun, nofifty, noten, nofive, notwo, noone, totalnotes ;

    printf ( "Enter the amount:\n" ) ;
    scanf ( "%d", &amt ) ;

    nohun = amt / 100 ;
    amt = amt % 100 ;
    nofifty = amt / 50 ;
    amt = amt % 50 ;
    noten = amt / 10 ;
    amt = amt % 10 ;
    nofive = amt / 5 ;
    amt = amt % 5 ;
    notwo = amt / 2 ;
    amt = amt % 2 ;
    noone = amt / 1 ;
    amt = amt % 1 ;

    totalnotes = nohun + nofifty + noten + nofive + notwo + noone ;

    printf ( "100 Rs. Notes = %d\n", nohun ) ;
    printf ( "50 Rs. Notes = %d\n", nofifty ) ;
    printf ( "10 Rs. Notes = %d\n", noten ) ;
    printf ( "5 Rs. Notes = %d\n", nofive ) ;
    printf ( "2 Rs. Notes = %d\n", notwo ) ;
    printf ( "1 Re. Notes = %d\n", noone ) ;
    printf ( "Smallest number of notes = %d\n", totalnotes ) ;

    return 0 ;
}
```

No of denominations = amount/denomination

Remainder = amount % denomination

## Sample Run

```
Enter the amount:
475
100 Rs. Notes = 4
50 Rs. Notes = 1
10 Rs. Notes = 2
5 Rs. Notes = 1
```

2 Rs. Notes = 0
1 Re. Notes = 0
Smallest number of notes = 8

## Explanation

/ operation gives the quotient, whereas % operator yields the remainder. So in the first step we find out how many hundreds are there in the **amt** value using /, and the balance amount using %. The same procedure is repeated for 50, 10, 5, 2 and 1.

## Challenge 07

Write a program to receive values of latitude (L1, L2) and longitude (G1, G2), in degrees, of two places on the earth and outputs the distance between them in nautical miles. The formula for distance in nautical miles is:

D = 3963 acos ( sin L1 sin L2 + cos L1cos L2 * cos ( G2 – G1 ) )

## Solution

```
/* Calculate distance between two places in Nautical Miles */
# include <stdio.h>
# include <math.h>

int main( )
{
    float lat1, lat2, lon1, lon2, d ;

    printf ( "Enter Latitude and Longitude of Place 1:\n" ) ;
    scanf ( "%f %f", &lat1, &lon1 ) ;

    printf ( "Enter Latitude and Longitude of Place 2:\n" ) ;
    scanf ( "%f %f", &lat2, &lon2 ) ;

    lat1 = lat1 * 3.14 / 180 ;
    lat2 = lat2 * 3.14 / 180 ;
    lon1 = lon1 * 3.14 / 180 ;
    lon2 = lon2 * 3.14 / 180 ;
```

```
d = 3963 * acos ( sin ( lat1 ) * sin ( lat2 ) + cos ( lat1 ) * cos ( lat2 )
    * cos ( lon2 - lon1 ) ) ;
printf ( "Dist. between Place1 & Place 2 = %f Nautical Miles\n", d ) ;

return 0 ;
}
```

## Sample Run

Enter Latitude and Longitude of Place 1:
21.14 79.08
Enter Latitude and Longitude of Place 2:
19.07 72.87
Dist. between Place 1 & Place 2 = 428.114990 Nautical Miles

## Explanation

The program uses the formula

D = 3963 acos ( sin L1 sin L2 + cos L1cos L2 * cos ( G2 – G1 ) )

to calculate the distance between two places in nautical miles. Note that to use the trigonometirc functions **sin( )**, **cos( )** and **acos( )** we need to include the file **math.h** at the beginning of the program.

# 02 / Total Challenges: 12

# Decision Making Challenges

If I get time, I would play Pokemon; if there is a good movie on TV I would stay at home; if I get a visa I would fly next month; if you do it so would I. Put all these statements in spotlight and you will notice that which action to take depends on certain condition being met. Often while writing a C program one has to perform different sets of actions depending on the satisfaction or failure of one or multiple conditions. Challenges 8 to 19 will show you how this is done.

## Challenge  08

Write a program to receive 5 numbers from keyboard and then report which is the biggest of the 5 numbers.

## Solution

```c
/* Biggest of 5 numbers */
#include <stdio.h>
int main( )
{
    int  i, j, k, l, m, big ;

    printf ( "Enter 5 numbers:\n" ) ;
    scanf ( "%d %d %d %d %d", &i, &j, &k, &l, &m ) ;

    big = i ;

    if ( j > big )
        big = j ;

    if ( k > big )
        big = k ;

    if ( l > big )
        big = l ;

    if ( m > big )
        big = m ;

    printf ( "Biggest Number = %d\n", big ) ;

    return 0 ;
}
```

## Sample Run

Enter 5 numbers:
56

32
65
78
2
Biggest Number = 78

## Explanation

The logic goes this way: Assume that the first number is the biggest number. Compare it with the second number. If the second number is bigger then store it in **big**, otherwise continue the comparison with thrid number. Repeat this process till we reach the fifth number.

## Challenge 09

Write a program to receive a character from keyboard and then determine whether the character entered is an upper case alphabet, lower case alphabet, digit or special symbol.

## Solution

```c
/* Determine type of character */
# include <stdio.h>
int main( )
{
    char  ch ;

    printf ( "Enter a character:\n" ) ;
    scanf ( "%c", &ch ) ;

    if ( ch >= 65 && ch <= 90 )
        printf ( "The character is an uppercase letter\n" ) ;

    if ( ch >= 97 && ch <= 122 )
        printf ( "The character is a lowercase letter\n" ) ;

    if ( ch >= 48 && ch <= 57 )
        printf ( "The character is a digit\n" ) ;
```

```
if ( ( ch >= 0 && ch < 48 ) || ( ch > 57 && ch < 65 )
   || ( ch > 90 && ch < 97 ) || ch > 122 )
   printf ( "The character is a special symbol\n" ) ;

return 0 ;
}
```

## Sample Runs

```
Enter a character:
4
The character is a digit

Enter a character:
*
The character is a special symbol

Enter a character:
R
The character is an uppercase letter

Enter a character:
b
The character is a lowercase letter
```

## Explanation

ASCII values of all characters lie in the range 0 to 255. There are different pre-assigned ranges for different types of characters. These are shown below:

| | |
|---|---|
| Uppercase letter | 65 to 90 |
| Lower case letter | 97 to 122 |
| Digit | 48 to 57 |
| Special symbol | 0 to 47, 58 to 64, 91 to 96, 123 to 255 |

So in the program we have received a character and checked in which out of the above ranges does its ASCII value lie. Accordingly, we have reported the type of the character.

You can do a better implementation of this program—using **if-else if-else** clause. This would be a better implementation because in the

*Note: If-else-if implementation is better suited*

current implementation, even if the first **if** is satisfied, rest of the **if**s are unnecessarily evaluated.

## Challenge 10

Write a program to receive values of a, b, c from a quadratic equation $ax^2 + bx + c = 0$ and determine its roots.

### Solution

```c
/* Roots of Quadratic equation */
#include <stdio.h>
#include <math.h>
int main( )
{
    float  a, b, c, disc, root1, root2 ;

    printf ( "Enter the coefficients (a, b and c):\n" ) ;
    scanf ( "%f %f %f", &a, &b, &c ) ;

    disc = b * b - 4.0 * a * c ;

    if ( disc < 0 )
        printf ( "No real roots\n" ) ;
    else
    {
        root1 = (-b + sqrt ( disc ) ) / ( 2.0 * a ) ;
        root2 = (-b - sqrt ( disc ) ) / ( 2.0 * a ) ;

        printf ( "Root 1 = %f\n", root1 ) ;
        printf ( "Root 2 = %f\n", root2 ) ;
    }
    return 0 ;
}
```

### Sample Runs

Enter the coefficients (a, b and c):
1

```
5
6
Root 1 = -2.000000
Root 2 = -3.000000

Enter the coefficients (a, b and c):
4
12
9
Root 1 = -1.500000
Root 2 = -1.500000

Enter the coefficients (a, b and c):
1
1
1
No real roots
```

## Explanation

On receiving the values of **a**, **b**, **c**, we have calculated the value of the discriminant. If discriminant is negative then the quadratic equation does not have real roots. If not, then we have calculated the two real roots and printed them.

## Challenge 11

If a year is input through the keyboard, write a program to determine whether the year is a leap year or not.

## Solution

```c
/* Check whether the year is leap or not */
# include <stdio.h>

int main( )
{
    int  yr ;
```

```
printf ( "Enter a year:\n" ) ;
scanf ( "%d", &yr ) ;

if ( yr % 100 == 0 )
{
    if ( yr % 400 == 0 )
        printf ( "Leap year\n" ) ;
    else
        printf ( "Not a Leap year\n" ) ;
}
else
{
    if ( yr % 4 == 0 )
        printf ( "Leap year\n" ) ;
    else
        printf ( "Not a leap year\n" ) ;
}

return 0 ;
}
```

If the
year divisible
by 100

↓

NO ———————— Yes

↓                    ↓

Check           check if
if               divisible
divisible           by
by               400
4

## Sample Runs

Enter a year:
1984
Leap Year

Enter a year:
2005
Not a Leap Year

Enter a year:
1800
Not a Leap Year

Enter a year:
2000
Leap Year

## Explanation

There is a simple rule for determining whether a year is leap or not. If the year is a century year and is divisible by 400 then it is a leap year. Also, if the year is a non-century year and is divisible by 4, then it is a leap year. In all other situations the year is not a leap year. The program just implements these conditions to test whether the given year is leap or not.

## Challenge  12

Given the coordinates **(x, y)** of center of a circle and its radius, write a program that will determine whether a point lies inside the circle, on the circle or outside the circle.

## Solution

```c
/* Determine position of point with respect to a circle */
#include <stdio.h>
#include <math.h>

int main( )
{
    float  centerX, centerY, radius ;
    float  pointX, pointY ;
    float  xDiff, yDiff ;
    float  distance ;

    printf ( "Enter coordinates of center of circle: \n" ) ;
    scanf ( "%f %f", &centerX, &centerY ) ;
    printf ( "Enter radius of circle: \n" ) ;
    scanf ( "%f", &radius ) ;

    printf ( "Enter coordinates of point: \n" ) ;
    scanf ( "%f %f", &pointX, &pointY ) ;

    xDiff = centerX - pointX ;
    yDiff = centerY - pointY ;
```

```
distance = sqrt ( ( xDiff * xDiff ) + ( yDiff * yDiff ) ) ;

if ( distance == radius )
    printf ("Point is on the circle\n" ) ;
else if ( distance < radius )
    printf ( "Point lies inside the circle\n" ) ;
else
    printf ( "Point lies outside the circle\n" ) ;

return 0 ;
}
```

## Sample Run

```
Enter coordinates of center of circle:
0
0
Enter radius of circle:
5
Enter coordinates of point:
5
0
Point is on the circle
```

## Explanation

The progam receives as input the coordinates of centre of circle and coordinates of the point in question. Then it determines the distance between these two points. Further it compares this distance with radius of the circle to determine whether the point lies inside, outside or on the circle.

## Challenge 13

If the three sides of a triangle are entered through the keyboard, write a program to check whether the triangle is isosceles, equilateral, scalene or right angled triangle.

## Solution

```c
/* Determine the type of triangle */
# include <stdio.h>
int main( )
{
    int  s1, s2, s3, a, b, c ;

    printf ( "Enter the sides of a triangle:\n" ) ;
    scanf ( "%d %d %d", &s1, &s2, &s3 ) ;

    if ( ( s1 + s2 <= s3 ) || ( s2 + s3 <= s1 ) || ( s1 + s3 <= s2 ) )
        printf ( "The sides do not form a triangle\n" ) ;
    else
    {
        if ( s1 != s2 && s2 != s3 && s3 != s1 )
            printf ( "Scalene triangle\n" ) ;

        if ( ( s1 == s2 ) && ( s2 != s3 ) )
            printf ( "Isosceles triangle\n" ) ;

        if ( ( s2 == s3 ) && ( s3 != s1 ) )
            printf ( "Isosceles triangle\n" ) ;

        if ( ( s1 == s3 ) && ( s3 != s2 ) )
            printf ( "Isosceles triangle\n" ) ;

        if ( s1 == s2 && s2 == s3 )
            printf ( "Equilateral triangle\n" ) ;

        a = ( s1 * s1 ) == ( s2 * s2 ) + ( s3 * s3 ) ;
        b = ( s2 * s2 ) == ( s1 * s1 ) + ( s3 * s3 ) ;
        c = ( s3 * s3 ) == ( s1 * s1 ) + ( s2 * s2 ) ;

        if ( a || b || c )
            printf ( "Right-angled triangle\n" ) ;
    }

    return 0 ;
}
```

*[handwritten annotation:]* None of the sides are equal

*[handwritten annotation:]* Only two sides are equal

## Sample Runs

```
Enter the sides of a triangle:
6   8   10
Scalene triangle
Right Angled Triangle

Enter the sides of a triangle:
3   3   3
Equilateral Triangle

Enter the sides of a triangle:
5   3   12
The sides do not form a triangle
```

## Explanation

First the program determines whether a triangle is valid or not. The triangle is valid only if sum of its two sides is greater than the third side. If the triangle is valid then it is determined whether the triangle is scalene (all sides unequal), isosceles (2 sides equal), equilateral (3 sides equal). To determine whether the triangle is a right angled triangle we have checked whether its sides form a Pythogorean triplet.

## Challenge 14

Given three points **(x1, y1)**, **(x2, y2)** and **(x3, y3)**, write a program to check if all the three points fall on one straight line.

## Solution

```c
/* Check whether three points are co-linear */
# include <stdio.h>
# include <math.h>
int main( )
{
    int  x1, y1, x2, y2, x3, y3 ;
    float  s1, s2, s3 ;
```

```
printf ( "\nEnter values of x1 and y1 coordinates of first point: " ) ;
scanf ( "%d%d", &x1, &y1 ) ;

printf ( "\nEnter values of x2 and y2 coordinates of first point: " ) ;
scanf ( "%d%d", &x2, &y2 ) ;

printf ( "\nEnter values of x3 and y3 coordinates of first point: " ) ;
scanf ( "%d%d", &x3, &y3 ) ;

if ( x1 == x2 && x2 == x3 )
    printf ( "Collinear\n" ) ;
else if ( x1 != x2 && x2 != x3 && x3 != x1 )
{
    /* Calculate Slope of line between each pair of points */
    s1 = ( float ) abs ( y2 - y1 ) / ( float ) abs ( x2 - x1 ) ;
    s2 = ( float ) abs ( y3 - y2 ) / ( float ) abs ( x3 - x2 ) ;
    s3 = ( float ) abs ( y3 - y1 ) / ( float ) abs ( x3 - x1 ) ;

    if ( s1 == s2 && s2 == s3 )
        printf ( "Collinear\n" ) ;
    else
        printf ( "Non Collinear\n" ) ;
}
else
    printf ( "Non Collinear\n" ) ;

return 0 ;
}
```

*Calculate Slope to determine if points fall in a Straight line* [handwritten annotation]

## Sample Runs

```
Enter values of x1 and y1 coordinates of first point: 4 5
Enter values of x2 and y2 coordinates of first point: 2 5
Enter values of x3 and y3 coordinates of first point: 3 5
Collinear

Enter values of x1 and y1 coordinates of first point: 1 1
Enter values of x2 and y2 coordinates of first point: 2 2
Enter values of x3 and y3 coordinates of first point: 3 3
Collinear
```

## Explanation

The three points would be collinear if the slopes of lines joining each pair of points are equal. While finding slopes there is a possibility that the denominator may turn out to be zero, hence before finding slopes it it necessary to ascertain that this is not the case.

## Challenge 15

Given a point **(x, y)**, write a program to find out if it lies on the x-axis, y-axis or on the origin.

## Solution

```c
/* Determine position of a point with respect to X and Y axes */
#include <stdio.h>
int main( )
{
    int  x, y ;

    printf ( "Enter the X and Y coordinates of the point:\n" ) ;
    scanf ( "%d %d", &x, &y ) ;

    if ( x == 0 && y == 0 )
        printf ( "Point is the origin\n" ) ;
    else if ( x == 0 && y != 0 )
        printf ( "Point lies on the Y axis\n" ) ;
    else if ( x != 0 && y == 0 )
        printf ( "Point lies on the X axis\n" ) ;
    else
    {
        if ( x > 0 && y > 0 )
            printf ( "Point lies in the First Quadrant\n" ) ;
        else if ( x < 0 && y > 0 )
            printf ( "Point lies in the Second Quadrant\n" ) ;
        else if ( x < 0 && y < 0 )
            printf ( "Point lies in the Third Quardant\n" ) ;
        else
```

```
        printf ( "Point lies in the Fourth Quadrant\n" ) ;
    }

    return 0 ;
}
```

```
Enter the X and Y coordinates of the point:
0   0
Point is the origin

Enter the X and Y coordinates of the point:
-10     -20
Point lies in the Third Quardant
```

## Explanation

In this program we have combined the usage of **if – else** with **if – else if – else** to determine the position of the point with respect to axes.

## Challenge 16

In boxing the weight class of a boxer is decided as per the following table. Write a program that receives weight as input and prints out the boxer's weight class.

| Boxer Class | Weight in Pounds |
|---|---|
| Flyweight | < 115 |
| Bantamweight | 115 - 121 |
| Featherweight | 122 - 153 |
| Middleweight | 154 – 189 |
| Heavyweight | >= 190 |

## Solution

```c
/* Decide Boxer class based on his weight */
#include <stdio.h>

int main( )
{
    int  weight ;

    printf ( "Enter weight in pounds:\n" ) ;
    scanf ( "%d", &weight ) ;

    if ( weight < 0 )
        printf ( "Invalid Input\n" ) ;
    else if ( weight >= 0 && weight < 115 )
        printf ( "Flyweight\n" ) ;
    else if ( weight >= 115 && weight < 122 )
        printf ( "Bantamweight\n" ) ;
    else if ( weight >= 122 && weight < 154 )
        printf ( "Featherweight\n" ) ;
    else if ( weight >= 154 && weight < 190 )
        printf ( "Middleweight\n" ) ;
    else
        printf ( "Heavyweight\n" ) ;

    return 0 ;
}
```

## Sample Runs

```
Enter weight in pounds:
130
Featherweight

Enter weight in pounds:
-76
Invalid Input
```

## Explanation

We have used **if – else if – else** instead of nested **if–else**s to determines the boxer's category. This makes the program easy to understand and maintain.

## Challenge 17

Write a program that receives month and date of birth as input and prints the corresponding Zodiac sign based on the following table:

| Zodiac Sign | From - To |
|---|---|
| Capricorn | December 22 - January 19 |
| Aquarius | January 20 - February 17 |
| Pisces | February 18 - March 19 |
| Aries | March 20 - April 19 |
| Taurus | April 20 - May 20 |
| Gemini | May 21 - June 20 |
| Cancer | June 21 - July 22 |
| Leo | July 23 - August 22 |
| Virgo | August 23 - September 22 |
| Libra | September 23 - October 22 |
| Scorpio | October 23 - November 21 |
| Sagittarius | November 22 - December 21 |

## Solution

```c
/* Decide Zodiac sign based on date and month of birth */
#include <stdio.h>
int main( )
{
    int  d, m ;

    printf ( "Enter day and month of birth:\n" ) ;
    scanf ( "%d %d", &d, &m ) ;

    if ( d <= 0 || m <= 0 )
```

```
            printf ( "Invalid Input\n" ) ;
      else if (((d >= 22 && d <= 31) && m == 12) || (d <= 19 && m == 1))
            printf ( "Capricorn \n" ) ;
      else if (((d >= 20 && d <= 31) && m == 1) || (d <= 17 && m == 2))
            printf ( "Aquarius\n" ) ;
      else if (((d >= 18 && d <= 29) && m == 2) || (d <= 19 && m == 3))
            printf ( "Pisces\n" ) ;
      else if (((d >= 20 && d <= 31) && m == 3) || (d <= 19 && m == 4))
            printf ( "Aries\n" ) ;
      else if (((d >= 20 && d <= 30) && m == 4) || (d <= 20 && m == 5))
            printf ( "Taurus\n" ) ;
      else if (((d >= 21 && d <= 31) && m == 5) || (d <= 20 && m == 6))
            printf ( "Gemini\n" ) ;
      else if (((d >= 21 && d <= 30) && m == 6) || (d <= 22 && m == 7))
            printf ( "Cancer\n" ) ;
      else if (((d >= 23 && d <= 31) && m == 7) || (d <= 22 && m == 8))
            printf ( "Leo\n" ) ;
      else if (((d >= 23 && d <= 31) && m == 8) || (d <= 22 && m == 9))
            printf ( "Virgo\n" ) ;
      else if (((d >= 23 && d <= 30) && m == 9) || (d <= 22 && m == 10))
            printf ( "Libra\n" ) ;
      else if (((d >= 23 && d <= 31) && m == 10) || (d <= 21 && m == 11))
            printf ( "Scorpio\n" ) ;
      else if (((d >= 22 && d <= 30) && m == 11) || (d <= 21 && m == 12))
            printf ( "Sagittarus\n" ) ;
      else
            printf ( "Invalid Input\n" ) ;

      return 0 ;
}
```

## Sample Runs

```
Enter day and month of birth:
32  12
Invalid Input

Enter day and month of birth:
22  3
Pisces
```
→ Aries

Enter day and month of birth:
28  12
Capricorn

## Explanation

The logic to determine the Zodiac sign is pretty straight-forward. Note that it is a good practice to validate the input before using it. For example, here we have ascertained that the value of **d** and **m** is not negative before using it to determine the Zodiac sign. If you wish, you can further check whether the value of **m** is greater than 12 and value of **d** is greater than 31. If yes, then the input is invalid.

## Challenge  18

An Electricity utility company charges its customers on the following basis depending on the category they belong to and the units that they have consumed for the month.

| Category | Fixed cost | Units consumed | Price |
|---|---|---|---|
| Residential | Rs. 50/mth for 1-phase meter<br>Rs. 200/mth for 3-phase meter | 0 to 100 units | Rs. 3.76 / unit |
| | | 101 to 300 units | Rs. 7.21 / unit |
| | | 301 to 500 units | Rs. 9.95 / unit |
| | | > 500 units | Rs. 11.31 / unit |
| Commercial | Rs. 220 / mth | 0 to 200 units | Rs. 6.60 / unit |
| | | > 200 units | Rs. 9.62 / unit |
| Industrial | Rs. 250 / mth | 0 to 20 KW | Rs. 5.43 / unit |
| | | > 20 KW | Rs. 6.88 / unit |
| Agricutural | Rs. 340 / mth | 0 to 5 HP | Rs. 258/HP/Mth |
| | | > 5 HP | Rs. 360/HP/Mth |

Write a program to calculate the monthly bill of the customer. Accept appropriate input for each category of consumer along with meter number.

## Solution

```c
/* Calculation of electricity bill */
#include <stdio.h>

int main( )
{
    int ch ;
    float price = 0 ;
    int wrongInput = 0 ;
    int meterType, numUnits, power ;

    printf ( "Choose the type of Customer:\n" ) ;
    printf ( "1. Residential\n" ) ;
    printf ( "2. Commercial\n" ) ;
    printf ( "3. Industrial\n" ) ;
    printf ( "4. Agricultural\n" ) ;
    printf ( "Enter your choice :\n" ) ;
    scanf ( "%d", &ch ) ;

    switch ( ch )
    {
        case 1 :
            printf ( "Enter type of meter:\n" ) ;
            printf ( "1. Single Phase Meter\n" ) ;
            printf ( "2. Three Phase Meter\n" ) ;
            printf ( "Enter your choice:\n" ) ;
            scanf ( "%d", &meterType ) ;

            switch ( meterType )
            {
                case 1 :
                    price = price + 50 ;
                    break ;
                case 2 :
```

```
            price = price + 200 ;
            break ;
        default :
            wrongInput = 1 ;
    }

    printf ( "Enter number of units consumed:\n" ) ;
    scanf ( "%d", &numUnits ) ;

    if ( numUnits >= 0 )
    {
        if ( numUnits <= 100 )
            price = price + numUnits * 3.76 ;
        else if ( numUnits > 100 && numUnits <= 300 )
            price = price + numUnits * 7.21 ;
        else if ( numUnits > 300 && numUnits <= 500 )
            price = price + numUnits * 9.95 ;
        else if ( numUnits > 500 )
            price = price + numUnits * 11.31 ;
    }
    else
        wrongInput = 1 ;
    break ;

case 2 :
    price = price + 220 ;
    printf ( "Enter number of units consumed:\n" ) ;
    scanf ( "%d", &numUnits ) ;

    if ( numUnits >= 0 )
    {
        if ( numUnits <= 200 )
            price = price + numUnits * 6.6 ;
        else
            price = price + numUnits * 9.62 ;
    }
    else
        wrongInput = 1 ;
    break ;

case 3 :
```

```
        price = price + 250 ;
        printf ( "Enter amount of power consumed:\n" ) ;
        scanf ( "%d", &power ) ;

        if ( power >= 0 )
        {
            if ( power <= 20 )
                price = price + power * 5.43 ;
            else
                price = price + power * 6.88 ;
        }
        else
            wrongInput = 1 ;
        break ;

    case 4 :
        price = price + 340 ;
        printf ( "Enter amount of horse power consumed:\n" ) ;
        scanf ( "%d", &power ) ;

        if ( power >= 0 )
        {
            if ( power <= 5 )
                price = price + power * 258 ;
            else
                price = price + power * 360 ;
        }
        else
            wrongInput = 1 ;
        break ;

    default :
        wrongInput = 1 ;
}

if ( wrongInput == 0 )
    printf ( "Total Electricity Bill = %f\n", price ) ;
else
    printf ( "Input not entered correctly\n" ) ;

return 0 ;
```

}

## Sample Run

Choose the type of Customer:
1. Residential
2. Commercial
3. Industrial
4. Agricultural
Enter your choice:
1
Enter type of meter:
1. Single Phase Meter
2. Three Phase Meter
Enter your choice:
2
Enter number of units consumed:
345
Total Electricity Bill = 3632.750000

## Explanation

When presented with choices, the program uses **switch** wherever branching has to be done based on the choice made by the user. At rest of the places it uses **if—else if—else** or **if—else** to do the decision-making.

## Challenge  19

In digital world colors are specified in Red-Green-Blue (RGB) format, with values of R, G, B varying on an integer scale from 0 to 255. In print publishing the colors are mentioned in Cyan-Magenta-Yellow-Black (CMYK) format, with values of C, M, Y, and K varying on a real scale from 0.0 to 1.0. Write a program that converts RGB color to CMYK color as per the following formulae:

$$White = Max(\text{Re}d\,/\,255, Green\,/\,255, Blue\,/\,255)$$

$$Cyan = \left(\frac{White - \text{Re}d\,/\,255}{White}\right)$$

$$Magenta = \left( \frac{White - Green/255}{White} \right)$$
$$Yellow = \left( \frac{White - Blue/255}{White} \right)$$

$$Black = 1 - White$$

Note that if the RGB values are all 0, then the CMY values are all 0 and the K value is 1.

## Solution

```
/* Color conversion from RGB to CMYK format */
# include <stdio.h>

int main( )
{
    float  red, green, blue ;
    float  white, cyan, magenta, yellow, black ;
    float  max ;

    printf ( "Enter Red, Green, Blue values (0 to 255):\n" ) ;
    scanf ( "%f %f %f", &red, &green, &blue ) ;

    if ( ( red < 0 || red > 255) || ( green < 0 || green > 255 ) ||
        ( blue < 0 || blue > 255 ) )
    {
        printf ( "Invalid RGB values\n" ) ;
        return 0 ;
    }

    if ( red == 0 && green == 0 && blue == 0 )
    {
        cyan = magenta = yellow = 0 ;
        black = 1 ;
    }
    else
    {
        red = red / 255.0 ;
        green = green / 255.0 ;
```

```
        blue = blue / 255.0 ;

        max = red ;
        if ( green > max )
            max = green ;
        if ( blue > max )
            max = blue ;

        white = max ;
        cyan = ( white - red ) / white ;
        magenta = ( white - green ) / white ;
        yellow = ( white - blue ) / white ;
        black = 1.0 - white ;
    }

    printf ( "CMYK = %f %f %f %f\n", cyan, magenta, yellow, black ) ;

    return 0 ;
}
```

## Sample Run

```
Enter Red, Green, Blue values (0 to 255):
200 140 245
CMYK = 0.183673 0.428571 0.000000 0.039216
```

## Explanation

The conversion formulae are used to convert RGB values to CMYK values. Note that even though R, G,, B values are integers, we still have defined **red**, **green** and **blue** as **float**s because if we keep them as integers, then division by 255 would fetch a 0, which we do not want.

# 03 / Total Challenges: 15

# Looping Challenges

The programming challenges that we faced so far needed either a sequential or a decision control instruction. These programs when executed always performed the same series of actions, in the same way, exactly once. In more complex programming situations we are required to perform an action over and over, often with variations in the details each time. This need is met by Loop Control Instruction, and is exemplified by Challenges 20 to 34.

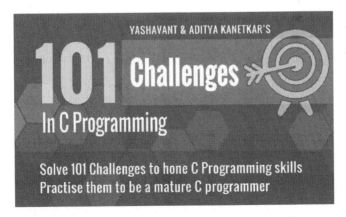

YASHAVANT & ADITYA KANETKAR'S

# 101 Challenges

## In C Programming

Solve 101 Challenges to hone C Programming skills
Practise them to be a mature C programmer

## Challenge 20

Here is an ecological simulation of wolf and rabbit populations. Rabbits eat grass. Wolves eat rabbits. There is plenty of grass, so wolves are the only obstacle to the rabbit population increase. The wolf population increases with the population of rabbits. The day-by-day changes in the rabbit population R and the wolf population W can be expressed by the following formulae:

R(tomorrow) = (1 + a).R(today) - c.R(today).W(today)

W(tomorrow) = (1 - b).W(today) + c.d.R(today).W(today)

a = 0.01 = fractional increase in rabbit population without threat from wolves ( 0.01 means 1 % increase)

b = 0.005 = fractional decrease in wolf population without rabbit to eat

c = 0.00001 = likelihood that a wolf will encounter and eat a rabbit

d = 0.01 = fractional increase in wolf population attributed to a devoured rabbit.

Assume that initially there are 10,000 rabbits and 1000 wolves. Write a program to calculate populations of rabbits and wolves over a 1000-day period. Have the program print the populations every 25 days. See what happens when you start with 500 wolves instead of 1000. Try starting with 2000 wolves too.

## Solution

```
/* Calculation of rabbit and wolf population */
#include <stdio.h>
int main( )
{
    float  a = 0.01, b = 0.005, c = 0.00001, d = 0.01 ;
    int  r1, w1, r2, w2 ;
    int  i ;

    printf ( "Enter initial rabbit and wolf population:\n" ) ;
    scanf ( "%d %d", &r1, &w1 ) ;
```

```
if ( r1 < 0 || w1 < 0 )
    printf ( "Initial population has to be non-negative. \n" ) ;
else
{
    for ( i = 1 ; i <= 1000 ; i++ )
    {
        r2 = ( 1 + a ) * r1 - c * r1 * w1 ;
        w2 = ( 1 - b ) * w1 + c * d * r1 * w1 ;

        if ( i % 25 == 0 )
            printf ( "After %d days R = %d W = %d\n", i, r2, w2 ) ;

        r1 = r2 ;
        w1 = w2 ;
    }
}
return 0 ;
}
```

## Sample Run

Enter initial rabbit and wolf population:
10000 2000
After 25 days, No of Rabbits = 7958 No of Wolves = 1800
After 50 days, No of Rabbits = 6654 No of Wolves = 1602
After 75 days, No of Rabbits = 5832 No of Wolves = 1427
After 100 days, No of Rabbits = 5337 No of Wolves = 1266
After 125 days, No of Rabbits = 5070 No of Wolves = 1116
After 150 days, No of Rabbits = 4988 No of Wolves = 990
After 175 days, No of Rabbits = 5063 No of Wolves = 869

... ... ... ...
... ... ... ...

## Explanation

Here **r1** and **w1** represent today's populations of rabbits and wolves respectively, whereas **r2** and **w2** represent their tomorrow's populations. Beginning with 10000 and 2000 as rabbits' and wolves' populations, through the **for** loop their tomorrow's populations are calculated using the formulae. The populations calculated are printed after a gap of 25 days. Whether 25 days are over is checked through the **if** statement within the **for** loop. The same program can be run with different initial values of **r1** and **w1**.

## Challenge 21

Write a program to generate all unique combinations of 1, 2 and 3 using **for** loops.

## Solution

```
/* Generate unique combinations of 1 2 3 */
# include <stdio.h>
int main( )
{
    int  i = 1, j = 1, k = 1 ;

    for ( i = 1 ; i <= 3 ; i++ )  /* 1st digit */
    {
        for ( j = 1 ; j <= 3 ; j++ )  /* 2nd digit */
        {
            for ( k = 1 ; k <= 3 ; k++ )  /* 3rd digit */
            {
                if ( i != j && j != k && k != i )
                    printf ( "%d%d%d\n", i , j , k ) ;
            }
        }
    }

    return 0 ;
}
```

*Handwritten annotations:*
*Figure out the iterative on pencil & paper*
*3 times*
*3 × 3 = 9*
*3 × 3 × 3 = 27*

## Sample Run

```
1 2 3
1 3 2
2 1 3
2 3 1
3 1 2
```

3 2 1

## Explanation

The three loops would generate all possible combinations of 1, 2 and 3. But these won't be unique combinations. For example, combinations 1 2 1 or 3 2 2 are not unique, as in the first combination 1 is repeated, whereas, in the second, 2 is being repeated. The **if** ensures that only unique combinations get printed out.

## Challenge  22

Write a program that finds four-digit perfect squares where the number represented by the first two digits and the number represented by the last two digits are also perfect squares.

## Solution

```c
#include <math.h>
#include <stdio.h>

int main( )
{
    int i, a, num, d1 , d2, d3, d4, nleft, nright, x, y ;

    for ( i = 1000 ; i <= 9999 ; i++ )
    {
        a = sqrt ( ( float ) i ) ;        — get sqrt of a number
        if ( i == a * a )                    check if it's a perfect square
        {
            num = i ;
            d4 = num % 10 ;     → Break the number
            num = num / 10 ;       down into its 4
            d3 = num % 10 ;        individual digits.
            num = num / 10 ;
            d2 = num % 10 ;
            num = num / 10 ;
            d1 = num % 10 ;
```

```
        nleft = d1 * 10 + d2 ;
        nright = d3 * 10 + d4 ;

        x = sqrt ( ( float ) nleft ) ;
        y = sqrt ( ( float ) nright ) ;

        if ( nleft == x * x && nright == y * y )
            printf ( "Desired number = %d\n", i ) ;
    }
}

    return 0 ;
}
```

→ Join first two digits

→ Join last two digits

## Sample Run

```
Desired number =1600
Desired number = 1681
Desired number = 2500
Desired number = 3600
Desired number = 4900
Desired number = 6400
Desired number = 8100
```

## Explanation

Inside the **for** loop, first we get the square root of **i** and test whether **i** is a perfect square or not. If it is a perfect square, then we segregate the four digits of this number into variables **d1, d2, d3** and **d4**. Next we construct two numbers **nleft** and **nright** from the first two and the last two digits of the four digit number. Having done this, we test whether these two numbers are perfect squares or not. If they turn out to be perfect squares then we have met the number satisfying our requirements. Hence we print it out. It is necessary to include the file "math.h" for the **sqrt( )** function to work.

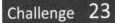

## Challenge 23

Write a program to print all prime numbers from 1 to 300.

## Solution

```c
/* Generate all prime numbers from 1 to 300 */
# include <stdio.h>
int main( )
{
    int  i, num = 1 ;

    printf ( "\nPrime numbers between 1 & 300 are:\n" ) ;
    printf ( "%d\t", num" ) ;

    while ( num <= 300 )
    {
        i = 2 ;
        while ( i <= num - 1 )
        {
            if ( num % i == 0 )
                break ;
            else
                i++ ;
        }

        if ( i == num )
            printf ( "%d\t", num ) ;

        num++ ;
    }

    return 0 ;
}
```

## Sample Run

```
1    2    3    5    7    11   13   17   19   23   29   31   37
41   43   47   53   59   61   67   71   73   79   83   89   97
.. .. .. ..
```

## Explanation

The program runs a for loop from 1 to 300 checking and printing all primes that it comes across. To check whether a number is prime or not, another for loop is used. In this loop if we check whether i is a factor of **num** using the expression **num % i == 0**. If this turns out to be true, we break out of the inner for loop. Otherwise, we increment i and try division with the incremented value. If no number from 2 to **num - 1** can divide **num** exactly it means that **num** is a prime number. If so found, we print the prime number and then go for the next number via the outer for loop.

## Challenge  24

Write a program to receive a positive integer and find its octal equivalent.

## Solution

```c
/* Find octal equivalent of a number */
# include <stdio.h>
# include <math.h>

int main( )
{
    int num, n, rem, oct, index;

    printf ( "Enter a non-negative decimal number:\n" ) ;
    scanf ( "%d", &num ) ;

    if ( num < 0 )
```

```
        printf ( "Invalid Input. \n" ) ;
    else
    {
        n = num ;
        oct = index = 0 ;

        while ( n > 0 )
        {
            rem = n % 8 ;
            n = n / 8 ;
            oct = oct + rem * pow ( 10, index ) ;
            index++ ;
        }

        printf ( "The octal equivalent of %d = %d\n", num, oct ) ;
    }
    return 0 ;
}
```

## Sample Runs

```
Enter a non-negative decimal number:
45
The octal equivalent of 45 = 55

Enter a non-negative decimal number:
77
The octal equivalent of 77 = 115
```

## Explanation

To obtain octal equivalent of an integer, we need to divide it continuously by 8 till dividend doesn't become zero, and then write the remainders obtained in reverse direction.

We cannot print the remainders as they are obtained, since the remainders are to be displayed in reverse order. So to construct a decimal number out of the remainders obtained, we have used the **pow( )** function to multiply each remainder obtained with increasing powers of 10, starting with 10 raised to 0.

*[Handwritten note in right margin:]* Note : How to derive octal equivalent of a decimal number

Challenge  **25**

The natural logarithm can be approximated by the following series.

$$\frac{x-1}{x}+\frac{1}{2}\left(\frac{x-1}{x}\right)^2+\frac{1}{3}\left(\frac{x-1}{x}\right)^3+\frac{1}{4}\left(\frac{x-1}{x}\right)^4+....$$

If **x** is input through the keyboard, write a program to calculate the sum of first seven terms of this series.

## Solution

```
/* Compute natural logarithm */
# include <stdio.h>
# include <math.h>
int main( )
{
    int  x, i ;
    float  term, result ;

    printf ( "Enter the value of x:\n" ) ;
    scanf ( "%d", &x ) ;

    if ( x <= 0 )
        printf ( "Log not defined\n" ) ;
    else
    {

        result = 0 ;
        for ( i = 1; i <= 7 ; i++ )
        {
            term = ( 1.0 / i ) * pow ( ( x - 1.0 ) / x, i ) ;
            result = result + term ;
        }

        printf ( "log ( %d ) = %f\n", x, result ) ;
    }

    return 0 ;
}
```

## Sample Runs

Enter the value of x: 3
log ( 3 ) = 1.086367

Enter the value of x: 2
log ( 2 ) = 0.692262

## Explanation

log of 0 and log of negative number are not defined. So first we need to validate the number whose log is to be obtained. If found valid, then we have obtained the sum of first seven terms of the series in the **for** loop. Since this is a running sum, we have to initialize **result** to a value 0, outside the loop.

## Challenge 26

Write a program to generate all Pythogorean Triplets with side length less than or equal to 20.

## Solution

```c
/* Generate Pythogorean Triplets */
#include <stdio.h>

int main( )
{
    int  i, j, k ;

    for ( i = 1 ; i <= 20 ; i++ )
    {
        for ( j = 1 ; j <= 20 ; j++ )
        {
            for ( k = 1 ; k <= 20 ; k++ )
            {
                if ( i * i + j * j == k * k )
```

```
                        printf ( "%d %d %d\n", i, j, k ) ;
                }
           }
     }

     return 0 ;
}
```

## Sample Run

```
3 4 5
4 3 5
5 12 13
6 8 10
8 6 10
8 15 17
9 12 15
12 5 13
12 9 15
12 16 20
15 8 17
16 12 20
```

## Explanation

Three sides of a traingle form a Pythogorean triplet if sum of squares of any two sides is equal to the square of the third side. We check this condition for all triangles by varying their sides from 1 to 20 through the **for** loops in turn.

## Challenge 27

The exponential function $e^x$ is defined as sum of the following series:

$$1+x-(x^2/2!)+(x^3/3!)+(x^4/4!)+\cdots$$

If **x** is input through the keyboard, write a program to calculate the sum of first ten terms of this series.

## Solution

```c
# include <stdio.h>
int main( )
{
    float  x ;
    int  i, j ;
    float  num, den, term, result ;

    printf ( "Enter the value of x:\n" ) ;
    scanf ( "%f", &x ) ;

    result = 0 ;
    for ( i = 1; i <= 10 ; i++ )
    {
        num = den = 1.0 ;
        for ( j = 1 ; j <= i ; j++ )
        {
            num = num * x ;
            den = den * j ;
        }
        term = num / den ;
        result = result + term ;
    }

    printf ( "exp = %f\n", result ) ;

    return 0 ;
}
```

## Sample Runs

```
Enter the value of x:
3
exp = 19.079666
```

```
Enter the value of x:
1.5
exp = 3.481687
```

## Explanation

This program calculates the value of each term in a **for** loop and keeps adding it to the running sum stored in **result**. The inner loop is used to caculate the numerator and denominator of each term by keeping their running products.

## Challenge 28

Write a program to find the factorial value of any number entered through the keyboard.

## Solution

```c
/* Calculation of factorial of any number */
# include <stdio.h>
int main( )
{
    int  num, i = 1 ;
    unsigned long int  fact = 1 ;

    /* factorial of 34 is beyond range of unsigned long int */
    printf ( "Enter any number (less than 34):\n" ) ;
    scanf ( "%d", &num ) ;

    while ( i <= num )
    {
        fact = fact * i ;
        i++ ;
    }
    printf ( "factorial of %d = %lu\n", num, fact ) ;

    return 0 ;
}
```

## Sample Runs

Enter any number (less than 34):

```
5
factorial of 5 = 120

Enter any number (less than 34):
7
factorial of 7 = 5040
```

## Explanation

Factorial for a given number is calculated using a running product stored in **fact**. It is necessary to initialize **fact** to a value 1.

## Challenge 29

Ramanujan number is the smallest number that can be expressed as sum of two cubes in two different ways. Write a program to print all such numbers up to a reasonable limit.

## Solution

```c
/* Generate numbers that satisfy Ramanujan numbers property */
#include <stdio.h>

int main( )
{
    int i, j, k, l ;

    for ( i = 1 ; i <= 30 ; i++ )
    {
        for ( j = 1 ; j <= 30 ; j++ )
        {
            for ( k = 1 ; k <= 30 ; k++ )
            {
                for ( l = 1 ; l <= 30 ; l++ )
                {
                    if ( ( i != j && i != k && i != l ) &&
                         ( j != i && j != k && j != l ) &&
                         ( k != i && k != j && k != l ) &&
```

Smallest Number which can be expressed as the Sum of two cubes in two different ways

```
                    ( l != i && l != j && l != k ) )
            {
                if ( i * i * i + j * j * j == k * k * k + l * l * l )
                    printf ( "%d\t%d\t%d\t%d\n", i, j, k, l ) ;
            }
          }
        }
      }
    }
}
```

## Sample Run

```
1729    1    12    9     10
1729    1    12    10    9
4104    2    16    9     15
4104    2    16    15    9
13832   2    24    18    20
13832   2    24    20    18
..  ..  ..  ..  ..
```

## Explanation

1729 is the smallest number that can be expressed as sum of two cubes in two different ways. i.e. $1729 = 1^3 + 12^3$ and $1729 = 9^3 + 10^3$.

The program runs 4 for loops and checks and prints other numbers that enjoy this property.

## Challenge  30

Write a program to print out all Armstrong numbers between 1 and 500. If sum of cubes of each digit of the number is equal to the number itself, then the number is called an Armstrong number. For example, 153 = ( 1 * 1 * 1 ) + ( 5 * 5 * 5 ) + ( 3 * 3 * 3 )

## Solution

```c
/* Generate all Armstrong numbers between 1 & 500 */
# include <stdio.h>
int main( )
{
    int  num, n, d1, d2, d3 ;
    printf ( "Armstrong numbers between 1 & 500 are:\n" ) ;

    for ( num = 1 ; num <= 500 ; num++ )
    {
        n = num ;
        d3 = n % 10 ;
        n = n / 10 ;
        d2 = n % 10 ;
        n = n / 10 ;
        d1 = n % 10 ;
        if ( ( d1 * d1 * d1 ) + ( d2 * d2 * d2 ) + ( d3 * d3 * d3 ) == num )
            printf ( "%d\n", num ) ;
    }

    return 0 ;
}
```

## Sample Run

```
Armstrong numbers between 1 & 500 are:
1
153
370
371
407
```

## Explanation

The program iterates through a loop from 1 to 500. Each time through the loop, it extracts individual digits of the number and checks whether they from an Amstrong number or not.

## Challenge  31

Write a program to produce the following output:

```
          1        1
     2        3      2 + 2
  4     5       6   2 + 2 + 2
7    8    9       10   2 + 2 + 2
```

## Solution

```c
/* Generate number pattern */
# include <stdio.h>

int main( )
{
    int  i, j, lines, spaces, num_in_a_line, num ;

    spaces = 20 ;
    num = 1 ;
    for ( lines = 1 ; lines <= 4 ; lines++ )
    {
        for ( i = 1 ; i <= spaces ; i++ )
            printf ( " " ) ;

        spaces -= 2 ;
        num_in_a_line = lines ;

        for ( j = 1 ; j <= num_in_a_line ; j++ )
        {
            printf ( " %d ", num ) ;
            num++ ;
        }
        printf ( "\n" ) ;
    }

    return 0 ;
}
```

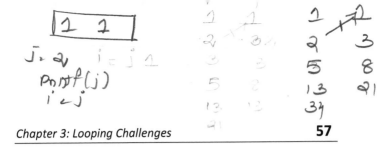

## Sample Run

```
      1
    2 3
   4 5 6
  7 8 9 10
```

## Explanation

In the pattern to be generated, the numbers to be printed increase from 1 onwards. Also, the number of numbers each line possesses is equal to the line number they belong to. For example, first line has one number, second line has two numbers and so on.

We have used three **for** loops here. The first loop controls the number of lines to be printed. The second prints the desired number of spaces in each line to obtain a traingular pattern. The third loop prints all the numbers that belong to a line.

## Challenge 32

Write a program to print first 20 terms of Fibonacci series.

## Solution

```c
/* Generate all prime numbers from 1 to 300 */
# include <stdio.h>
int main( )
{
    int old, new, i, newterm ;

    old = 1 ;
    new = 1 ;

    printf ( "%d\n", old ) ;
    printf ( "%d\n", new ) ;
```

```
for ( i = 3 ; i <= 20 ; i++ )
{
    newterm = old + new ;
    printf ( "%d\n", newterm ) ;
    old = new ;
    new = newterm ;
}

return 0 ;
}
```

## Sample Run

```
1
1
2
3
5
8
13
21
..
..
```

## Explanation

First two terms of a Fibonacci series are 1 and 1. The rest of the terms are such that their value is sum of two terms pervious to it. Thus 2 is 1 + 1, 3 is 1 + 2, 5 is 2 + 3, etc. Since there is no logic to generate the first two terms, their values are printed without generating their values. The rest of the terms of the series are generated and printed through the **for** loop.

## Challenge   33

When interest compounds **q** times per year at an annual rate of **r** % for **n** years, the principal **p** compounds to an amount **a** as per the following formula

$$a = p \left( 1 + r / q / 100 \right)^{nq}$$

Write a program to read 10 sets of **p, r, n & q** and calculate the corresponding **a**s.

## Solution

```c
/* Compound interest calculation */
# include <stdio.h>
# include <math.h>
int main( )
{
    float  q, r, n, p, a ;
    int  i ;

    for ( i = 1 ; i < 10 ; i++ )
    {
        printf ( "Enter the principal amount:\n" ) ;
        scanf ( "%f", &p ) ;
        printf ( "Enter the rate of interest:\n" ) ;
        scanf ( "%f", &r ) ;
        printf ( "Enter the number of years:\n" ) ;
        scanf ( "%f", &n ) ;
        printf ( "Enter the compounding period:\n" ) ;
        scanf ( "%f", &q ) ;

        a = p * pow ( ( 1 + ( r / q / 100 ) ), ( n * q ) ) ;

        printf ( "Total amount = %f\n\n", a ) ;
    }

    return 0 ;
}
```

## Sample Run

Enter the principal amount:
1000
Enter the rate of interest:
7.5

Enter the number of years:
15003
Enter the compounding period:
1
Total amount = 1242.296875

Enter the principal amount:
15000
Enter the rate of interest:
12
Enter the number of years:
4
Enter the compounding period:
2
Total amount = 23907.720703
.. .. .. ..
.. .. .. ..

## Explanation

The program is pretty stright-forward. It receives the values of of **p, r, n** & **q** and calculates the corresponding amounts in a loop that runs around 10 times.

 ## Challenge 34

Write a program to print 24 hours of day with suitable suffixes like AM, PM, Noon and Midnight.

## Solution

```c
/* Print hours of the day with suitable suffixes */
#include <stdio.h>

int main( )
{
    int hour ;
```

```
for ( hour = 0 ; hour <= 23 ; hour++ )
{
    if ( hour == 0 )
    {
        printf ( "12 Midnight\n" ) ;
        continue ;
    }

    if ( hour < 12 )
        printf ( "%d AM\n", hour ) ;

    if ( hour == 12 )
        printf ( "12 Noon\n" ) ;

    if ( hour > 12 )
        printf ( "%d PM\n", hour % 12 ) ;

}

    return 0 ;
}
```

## Sample Run

```
12 Midnight
1 AM
2 AM
3 AM
4 AM
.. ..
.. ..
11 AM
12 Noon
1 PM
2 PM
3 PM
4 PM
.. ..
.. ..
10 PM
11 PM
```

## Explanation

The program runs a **for** loop for 24 hours and then based on the value of hour outputs an appropriate message.

# 04 / Total Challenges: 6

# Function Challenges

A function is a self-contained block of statements that perform a coherent task of some kind. Every C program is a collection of one or more functions. It is also possible to carry out communication between these functions using parameters and return values. This chapter presents challenges related with functions and their communication.

## Challenge 35

Write a general-purpose function to convert any given year into its roman equivalent. Use the following roman equivalents for decimal numbers:

1 – I, 5 – V, 10 – X, 50 – L, 100 – C, 500 – D, 1000 – M.

Example:

Roman equivalent of 1988 is mdccclxxxviii
Roman equivalent of 1525 is mdxxv

## Solution

```c
/* Convert given year into its roman equivalent */
# include <stdio.h>

int romanise ( int, int, char ) ;
int main( )
{
    int  yr ;

    printf ( "Enter  year:\n" ) ;
    scanf ( "%d", &yr ) ;

    yr = romanise ( yr, 1000, 'm' ) ;
    yr = romanise ( yr, 500, 'd' ) ;
    yr = romanise ( yr, 100, 'c' ) ;
    yr = romanise ( yr, 50, 'l' ) ;
    yr = romanise ( yr, 10, 'x' ) ;
    yr = romanise ( yr, 5, 'v' ) ;
    yr = romanise ( yr, 1, 'i' ) ;

    return 0 ;
}

int romanise ( int y, int k, char ch )
{
    int  i, j ;
```

```
if ( y == 4 )
{
    printf ( "iv" ) ;
    return ( y % 4 ) ;
}

if ( y == 9 )
{
    printf ( "ix" ) ;
    return ( y % 9 ) ;
}

if ( y == 49 )
{
    printf ( "il" ) ;
    return ( y % 49 ) ;
}

if ( y == 99 )
{
    printf ( "ic" ) ;
    return ( y % 99 ) ;
}

if ( y == 499 )
{
    printf ( "id" ) ;
    return ( y % 499 ) ;
}

if ( y == 999 )
{
    printf ( "im" ) ;
    return ( y % 999 ) ;
}

j = y / k ;

for ( i = 1 ; i <= j ; i++ )
    printf ( "%c", ch ) ;
```

```
        return ( y % k ) ;
}
```

## Sample Runs

```
Enter year:
19
xix
```

```
Enter year:
1998
mdcccclxxxxviii
```

## Explanation

**romanise( )** is a generic function which finds out in **y** how many times **k** occurs and prints out **ch** those many times. For example, if the value of year is 1998, then during the first call **romanise( )** finds out in 1998 how many times 1000 occurs and prints out 'm' those many times.

**romanise( )** uses several **if** statements to take care of special cases of years like 4, 49, 99, 499 and 999.

## Challenge  36

Write a program to receive two integers from the keyboard and obtain LCM and GCD of these two numbers through functions **lcm( )** and **gcd( )**.

## Solution

```c
/* Obtain LCM and GCD of two numbers */
# include <stdio.h>

int lcm ( int, int ) ;
int gcd ( int, int ) ;

int main( )
{
    int  num1, num2 ;
```

```
    int l, g ;

    printf ( "Enter two positive integers:\n" ) ;
    scanf ( "%d %d", &num1, &num2 ) ;

    l = lcm ( num1, num2 ) ;
    g = gcd ( num1, num2 ) ;
    printf ( "LCM = %d GCD = %d", l, g ) ;

    return 0 ;
}

int lcm ( int n1, int n2 )
{
    int z ;

    /* store maximum out of n1 and n2 in z */
    z = n1 > n2 ? n1 : n2 ;

    while ( 1 )
    {
        if( z % n1 == 0 && z % n2 == 0 )
            break ;

        z++ ;
    }
    return ( z ) ;
}

int gcd ( int n1, int n2 )
{
    int i, z ;

    for ( i = 1 ; i <= n1 ; i++ )
    {
        if ( n1 % i == 0 && n2 % i == 0 )
            z = i ;
    }

    return ( z ) ;
}
```

## Sample Runs

```
Enter two positive integers:
4 5
LCM = 20 GCD = 1

Enter two positive integers:
12 15
LCM = 60 GCD = 3
```

## Explanation

The **lcm( )** function firstly stores the larger number among **n1** and **n2** in **z**. The LCM of two numbers cannot be less than **z**. Then in an infinite **while** loop in each iteration it is checked whether **z** is perfectly divisible by **n1** and **n2**. If this test condition is not true, **z** is incremented by 1 and the iteration continues until the test expression of **if** statement is true. Final value in z is the LCM of the two numbers.

The **gcd( )** function finds in a loop, any number starting with 1 that can divide **n1** and **n2** exactly. The greatest such number is the greatest common divisor of the two numbers **n1** and **n2**.

The LCM of two numbers could also have been found using the formula:

LCM = ( num1 * num2 ) / GCD.

## Challenge 37

Write a program that receives coordinates of the top left corner of a rectangle, its width and height and coordinates of a point. Write a function that determines whether the point lies inside, outside or on the rectangle.

## Solution

```c
/* Determine position of point w.r.t. a rectangle */
#include <stdio.h>
```

```
int PointInRect ( int, int, int, int, int, int ) ;

int main( )
{
    int  x1, y1, wd, ht, xpt, ypt ;
    int  pos ;

    printf ( "Enter x1, y1, width and height of rectangle:\n" ) ;
    scanf ( "%d %d %d %d", &x1, &y1, &wd, &ht ) ;

    printf ( "Enter coordinates of point:\n" ) ;
    scanf ( "%d %d", &xpt, &ypt ) ;

    pos = PointInRect ( x1, y1, wd, ht, xpt, ypt ) ;

    switch ( pos )
    {
        case 1 :
            printf ( "Point lies outside the rectangle" ) ;
            break ;
        case 2 :
            printf ( "Point lies inside the rectangle" ) ;
            break ;
        case 3 :
            printf ( "Point lies on the rectangle" ) ;
            break ;
    }

    return 0 ;
}

int PointInRect ( int  x1, int  y1, int  wd, int  ht, int  xpt, int  ypt )
{
    int  x2, y2 ;

    x2 = x1 + wd ;
    y2 = y1 + ht ;

    if ( xpt < x1 || xpt > x2 || ypt < y1 || ypt > y2 )
        return 1 ;
```

```
        if ( xpt > x1 && xpt < x2 && ypt > y1 && ypt < y2 )
            return 2 ;

        return 3 ;
    }
```

## Sample Runs

```
Enter x1, y1, width and height of rectangle:
0 0 10 20
Enter coordinates of point:
5 5
Point lies inside the rectangle

Enter x1, y1, width and height of rectangle:
10 20 30 50
Enter coordinates of point:
10 35
Point lies on the rectangle

Enter x1, y1, width and height of rectangle:
15 15 30 30
Enter coordinates of point:
5 10
Point lies outside the rectangle
```

## Explanation

The function **PointInRect( )** handles the three cases of point being outside, inside or on the rectangle. Note the order in which these cases are tackled. If the order is changed we would be required to check several conditions to determine whether the point lies on the rectangle or not.

 ## Challenge 38

Write a program that receives two numbers in **a** and **b** and then calls the function **power ( a, b )**, to calculate the value of **a** raised to **b**.

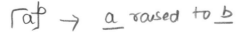

## Solution

```c
/* Calculate one number raised to the power of another */
#include <stdio.h>
float power ( float, int ) ;

int main ( )
{
    float a ;
    int b ;
    float result ;

    printf ( "Enter the number and the exponent: \n" ) ;
    scanf ( "%f %d", &a, &b ) ;

    result = power ( a, b ) ;
    printf ( "Result = %f\n", result ) ;

    return 0 ;
}

float power ( float n, int exponent )
{
    int absexp, i ;
    float prod ;

    if ( exponent == 0 )
        return 1.0 ;
    else
    {
        if ( exponent < 0 )
            absexp = exponent * ( -1 ) ;
        else
            absexp = exponent ;

        prod = 1.0 ;
        for ( i = 1 ; i <= absexp ; i++ )
            prod = prod * n ;

        if ( exponent < 0 )
```

```
        prod = 1.0 / prod ;

    return ( prod ) ;
    }
}
```

## Sample Runs

```
Enter the number and the exponent:
2 5
Result = 32.000000

Enter the number and the exponent:
2 -5
Result = 0.031250
```

## Explanation

The function power( ) takes into account cases like exponent being zero, negative or positive. If the exponent is non-zero then it calculates the running product to obtain the value of **a** raised to **b** (or **n** raised to **exponent**). It appropriately returns this product or its reciprocal depending upon whether the exponent is positive or negative.

*Index it*

## Challenge 39

A positive integer is entered through the keyboard. Write a function to obtain the prime factors of this number.

For example, prime factors of 24 are 2, 2, 2 and 3, whereas prime factors of 35 are 5 and 7.

## Solution

```c
/* Obtain prime factors of a number */
# include <stdio.h>
void prime ( int ) ;

int main( )
{
```

```
    int  num ;

    printf ( "Enter number:\n" ) ;
    scanf ( "%d", &num ) ;

    if ( num < 2 )
        printf ( "Invalid Input\n" ) ;
    else
        prime ( num ) ;

    return 0 ;
}

void prime ( int num )
{
    int  i = 2 ;

    printf ( "Prime factors of %d are: ", num ) ;
    while ( num != 1 )
    {
        if ( num % i == 0 )
            printf ( "%d ", i ) ;
        else
        {
            i++ ;
            continue ;
        }
        num = num / i ;
    }
}
```

## Sample Runs

```
Enter number:
24
Prime factors of 24 are: 2 2 2 3

Enter number:
45
Prime factors of 45 are: 3 3 5
```

## Explanation

The **prime( )** function checks in a loop whether the **num** is divisible by 2, 3, 4, etc. Any time it finds **num** to be perfectly divisible, it prints that factor ( i ) and reduces **num** to **num / i.** It continues to do this till **num** reaches 1.

## Challenge 40

Write a program to generate Pascal's Triangle pattern shown below:

```
      1
     1 1
    1 2 1
   1 3 3 1
  1 4 6 4 1
 1 5 10 10 5 1
```

## Solution

```c
/* Generate Pascal Triangle pattern */
#include <stdio.h>
int fact ( int ) ;

int main( )
{
    int i, l, num = 5 ;

    for ( l = 0 ; l <= num ; l++ )
    {
        for ( i = 0 ; i <= ( num - l - 1 ) ; i++ )
            printf ( " " ) ;

        for ( i = 0 ; i <= l ; i++ )
            printf ( "%d  ", fact ( l ) / ( fact ( i ) * fact ( l - i ) ) ) ;
        printf ( "\n" ) ;
    }

    return 0 ;
```

*(handwritten annotations:)*
Index 74

LOOP controls Line NO →

Loop controls space →

Loop controls Printing numbers on each line →

```
}

int  fact ( int  n )
{
    int  i, p ;

    p = 1 ;
    for ( i = 1; i <= n ; i++)
        p = p * i ;

    return p ;
}
```

## Sample Run

```
        1
      1  1
    1  2  1
   1  3  3  1
  1  4  6  4  1
 1  5  10  10  5  1
```

## Explanation

From the pattern of Pascal's triangle one can note that number of entries in each line is same as line number to which they belong. For example, first line has 1 entry, second line has 2 entries and so on.

Each $i^{th}$ entry in $l^{th}$ line is obtained using the formula

$l ! / ( ( l - i ) ! * i !$

To obtain the factorial values in this formula we have called the **fact( )** function thrice, each time passing it a different argument.

The outer **for** loop controls the number of lines to be printed in the pattern. Out of the two inner **for** loops, the first one prints the spaces, whereas the second prints the numbers in a particular line.

# 05 / Total Challenges: 4

# Pointer Challenges

Thorough knowledge of pointers is what separates men from boys. This chapter presents simple challenges regarding pointers and their usage. More rigorous pointers challenges would be presented in chapters on Arrays, Strings, Structures and IO.

## Challenge 41

If five numbers are received from the keyboard, write a function that would calculate their sum, product and average. Print these results in **main ( )**.

### Solution

```
/* Calculate sum, product, average of 5 numbers */
# include <stdio.h>
void cal_spa ( int, int, int, int, int, int *, int *, int * ) ;

int main ( )
{
    int num1, num2, num3, num4, num5 ;
    int sum, prod, avg ;

    printf ( "Enter 5 numbers:\n" ) ;
    scanf ( "%d %d %d %d %d", &num1, &num2,
            &num3, &num4, &num5 ) ;

    cal_spa ( num1, num2, num3, num4, num5, &sum, &prod, &avg ) ;

    printf ( "Sum = %d\n", sum ) ;
    printf ( "Product = %d\n", prod ) ;
    printf ( "Average = %d\n", avg ) ;

    return 0 ;
}

void cal_spa ( int n1, int n2, int n3, int n4, int n5, int *s, int *p, int *a )
{
    *s = n1 + n2 + n3 + n4 + n5 ;
    *p = n1 * n2 * n3 * n4 * n5 ;
    *a = *s / 5 ;
}
```

## Sample Run

```
Enter 5 numbers:
3 5 8 12 15
Sum = 43
Product = 21600
Average = 8
```

## Explanation

We have received and passed 5 numbers to **cal_spa( )**. Along with them we have also passed addresses of **sum, prod, avg**. How do do we decide which variable's value should be passed and which variable's address should be passed? Simple. If we want to change the variable through the called function we should pass its address, otherwise we should pass its value. We wanted to change values of **sum, prod** and **avg** through **cal_spa( )**, so we passed their addresses to it.

## Challenge 42

If the lengths of the sides of a triangle are denoted by **a, b**, and **c**, then area of triangle is given by

$$area = \sqrt{S(S-a)(S-b)(S-c)}$$

where, $S = (a + b + c) / 2$.

Write a program that receives three sides of a triangle and calculates its area and perimeter through a function.

## Solution

```c
/* Calculate area and perimeter of a triangle */
# include <stdio.h>
# include <math.h>
void cal_areaperi ( float, float, float, float *, float * ) ;

int main( )
{
```

*Pass by value*
*V/s*
*Pass by reference*

*If we want to change a variable's value through the function we called, we pass the variable's address*

```
    float  s1, s2, s3, area, peri ;

    printf ( "Enter three sides of the triangle:\n" ) ;
    scanf ( "%f%f%f", &s1, &s2, &s3 ) ;

    cal_areaperi ( s1, s2, s3, &area, &peri ) ;
```

*Addresses Passed*

```
    printf ( "Area of the triangle = %f\n", area ) ;
    printf ( "Perimeter of the triangle = %f\n", peri ) ;

    return 0 ;
}

void cal_areaperi ( float s1, float s2, float s3, float *a, float *p )
{
    float  s ;

    s = ( s1 + s2 + s3 ) / 2 ;
    *a = sqrt ( s * ( s - s1 ) * ( s - s2 ) * ( s - s3 ) ) ;
    *p = s1 + s2 + s3 ;
}
```

## Sample Run

```
Enter three sides of the triangle:
3 4 5
Area of the triangle = 6.000000
Perimeter of the triangle = 12.000000
```

## Explanation

We have passed **s1, s2, s3** by value and area, **peri** by reference. This is because we wish to change the values of **area** and **peri** through the function **cal_areaperi( )**.

## Challenge  43

Write a function that receives 5 integers and returns the sum, average and standard deviation of these numbers. Call this function from **main( )**

and print the results in **main( )**.

## Solution

```
/* Calculates sum, average and standard deviation */
# include <stdio.h>
# include <math.h>
void cal_sasd ( int, int, int, int, int, float *, float *, float * ) ;

int main( )
{
    int  n1, n2, n3, n4, n5 ;
    float  sum, avg, stddev ;

    printf ( "Enter 5 numbers:\n" ) ;
    scanf ( "%d%d%d%d%d", &n1, &n2, &n3, &n4, &n5 ) ;

    cal_sasd ( n1, n2, n3, n4, n5, &sum, &avg, &stddev ) ;

    printf ( "Sum = %f\n", sum ) ;
    printf ( "Average = %f\n", avg ) ;
    printf ( "Standard deviation = %f\n", stddev ) ;

    return 0 ;
}

void  cal_sasd ( int  n1, int  n2, int  n3, int  n4, int  n5,
                 float  *s, float  *a, float  *sd )
{
    *s = n1 + n2 + n3 + n4 + n5 ;
    *a = *s / 5 ;
    *sd = sqrt ( ( pow ( ( n1 - *a ), 2 ) + pow ( ( n2 - *a ), 2 ) +
                   pow ( ( n3 - *a ), 2 ) + pow ( ( n4 - *a ), 2 ) +
                   pow ( ( n5 - *a ), 2 ) ) / 4 ) ;
}
```

→ Should be 5

## Sample Run

Enter 5 numbers:

```
4 5 3 7 9
Sum = 28.000000
Average = 5.600000
Standard deviation = 2.408319
```

## Explanation

This program is similar to challenges and their explanations presented in Challenge 41 and 42.

## Challenge 44

Write a function to compute the distance between two points and use it to develop another function that will compute the area of the triangle whose vertices are **A ( x1, y1 )**, **B ( x2, y2 )**, and **C ( x3, y3 )**, if the triangle is a valid triangle.

## Solution

```c
/* Calculate area of triangle */
#include <stdio.h>
#include <math.h>

float  distance ( int, int, int, int ) ;
int  isTriangleValid ( float, float, float ) ;
float  areaOfTriangle ( float, float, float ) ;

int main( )
{
    int  x1, y1, x2, y2, x3, y3 ;
    float  s1, s2, s3, area ;
    int  isValid = 0 ;

    printf ( "Enter the coordinates of 3 vertices of the triangle: \n" ) ;
    printf ( "First Vertex ( x, y ): \n" ) ;
    scanf ( "%d %d", &x1, &y1 ) ;
    printf ( "Second Vertex ( x, y ): \n" ) ;
    scanf ( "%d %d", &x2, &y2 ) ;
    printf ( "Third Vertex ( x, y ): \n" ) ;
```

```
    scanf ( "%d %d", &x3, &y3 ) ;

    s1 = distance ( x1, y1, x2, y2 ) ;
    s2 = distance ( x2, y2, x3, y3 ) ;
    s3 = distance ( x1, y1, x3, y3 ) ;

    printf ( "Length of first side = %f\n", s1 ) ;
    printf ( "Length of second side = %f\n", s2 ) ;
    printf ( "Length of third side = %f\n", s3 ) ;

    isValid = isTriangleValid ( s1, s2, s3 ) ;
    if ( isValid )
    {
        area = areaOfTriangle ( s1, s2, s3 ) ;
        printf ( "Area: %f\n", area ) ;
    }
    else
        printf ( "The three sides do not form a triangle. \n" ) ;
    return 0 ;
}

int isTriangleValid ( float s1, float s2, float s3 )
{
    if ( s1 <= 0 || s2 <= 0 || s3 <= 0 )
        return 0 ;
    else if ( ( s1 + s2 <= s3 ) || ( s2 + s3 <= s1 ) || ( s1 + s3 <= s2 ) )
        return 0 ;
    else
        return 1 ;
}

float areaOfTriangle ( float s1, float s2, float s3 )
{
    float s ;

    s = ( s1 + s2 + s3 ) / 2.0 ;
    return sqrt ( s * ( s - s1 ) * ( s - s2 ) * ( s - s3 ) ) ;
}

float distance ( int x1, int y1, int x2, int y2 )
{
```

```
    float  sq ;

    sq = ( x2 - x1 ) * ( x2 - x1 ) + ( y2 - y1 ) * ( y2 - y1 ) ;
    return  sqrt ( sq ) ;
}
```

## Sample Run

```
First Vertex ( x, y ):
0 0
Second Vertex ( x, y ):
6 0
Third Vertex ( x, y ):
0 8
Length of first side = 6.000000
Length of second side = 10.000000
Length of third side = 8.000000
Area: 24.000000
```

## Explanation

Given the three vertices, the program calls **distance( )** to obtain length of three sides joining these vertices. Then it calls **isTriangleValid( )** to check whether the three sides form a valid triangle or not. If they do, then it calls **areaOfTriangle( )** to calculate the area of the triangle using Heron's formula.

Heron's formula when three sides of a triangle are known

# 06 / Total Challenges: 8

# Recursion Challenges

**R**ecursion is perhaps the toughest nut to crack in C programming. There are lots of places where this feature of functions is useful. This chapter presents many challenges that make you use recursion to perform useful tasks.

✓ ## Challenge 45

*Index it of*
*Tower Hanoi*

There are three pegs labeled A, B and C. Four disks are placed on peg A. The bottom-most disk is largest, and disks go on decreasing in size with the topmost disk being smallest. The objective of the game is to move the disks from peg A to peg C, using peg B as an auxiliary peg. The rules of the game are as follows:

(a) Only one disk may be moved at a time, and it must be the top disk on one of the pegs.

(b) A larger disk should never be placed on the top of a smaller disk.

Write a program to print out the sequence in which the disks should be moved such that all disks on peg A are finally transferred to peg C.

## Solution

```c
/* Towers of Hanoi */
#include <stdio.h>
void move ( int, char, char, char ) ;

int main( )
{
    int n = 4 ;
    move ( n, 'A', 'B', 'C' ) ;
    return 0 ;
}

void move ( int n, char sp, char ap, char ep )
{
    if ( n == 1 )
        printf ( "Move from %c to %c\n", sp, ep ) ;
    else
    {
        move ( n - 1, sp, ep, ap ) ;
        move ( 1, sp,' ', ep ) ;
        move ( n - 1, ap, sp, ep ) ;
    }
}
```

A, C

(A, C, B)
CA, ' ', C)
( B, A, C)

*Base case*

move n-1 from A to B
move last disk from A to C
move n-1 from B to A

## Sample Run

Move from A to B
Move from A to C
Move from B to C
Move from A to B
Move from C to A
Move from C to B
Move from A to B
Move from A to C
Move from B to C
Move from B to A
Move from C to A
Move from B to C
Move from A to B
Move from A to C
Move from B to C

## Explanation

This problem is the famous Towers of Hanoi problem, wherein three pegs are to be employed for transferring the disks with the given rules. Here's how we go about it. We have three pegs: the starting peg, **sp**, the auxiliary peg **ap**, and the ending peg, **ep**, where the disks must finally be. First, using the ending peg as an auxiliary or supporting peg, we transfer all but the last disk to **ap**. Next the last disk is moved from **sp** to **ep**. Now, using **sp** as the supporting peg, all the disks are moved from **ap** to **ep**.

The three pegs are denoted by 'A', 'B' and 'C'. The recursive function **move( )** is called with different combinations of these pegs as starting, auxiliary and ending pegs. Going through the following figure would be the best way to sort out how the control flows through the program.

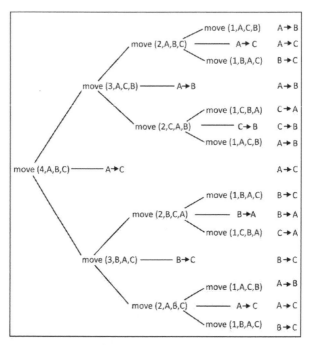

Figure 6.1. *Towers of Hanoi for 4 Disks.*

## Challenge 46

If a positive integer is entered through the keyboard, write a recursive function to obtain the prime factors of the number.

## Solution

```
/* Find Prime Factors of a number recursively */
# include <stdio.h>

void factorise ( int, int ) ;
int main( )
{
```

```
    int  num ;

    printf ( "Enter a number:\n" ) ;
    scanf ( "%d", &num ) ;

    printf ( "Prime factors are:\n" ) ;
    factorise ( num, 2 ) ;
    return 0 ;
}

void factorise ( int  n, int  i )
{
    if ( i <= n )
    {
        if ( n % i == 0 )
        {
            printf ( "%d ", i ) ;
            n = n / i ;
        }
        else
            i++ ;

        factorize ( n, i ) ;
    }
}
```

Handwritten annotations:
- if ( i <= n ) → Base case as long as i < = n
- if ( n % i == 0 ) → If evenly divisble
- printf ( "%d ", i ) ; Print the number
- n = n / i ; reduce the number by the factor

## Sample Run

```
Enter a number:
42
Prime factors are:
2 3 7
```

## Explanation

Since the samllest prime factor that a number can have is 2, while calling **factorise( )**, in addition to **num** we have also passed 2. In **factorize( )** we keep checking, starting with 2, whether **i** is a factor of **n** (means, can **i** divide **n** exactly). If so, we print that factor, reduce **n** and again call

**factorize( )** recursively. If not, we increment **i** and call **factorize( )** to check whether the new **i** is a factor of **n**.

## Challenge 47

A positive integer is entered through the keyboard, write a recursive function to calculate sum of digits of the 5-digit number.

### Solution

```c
/* Recursive sum of digits of a positive integer */
# include <stdio.h>
int rsum ( int ) ;

int main( )
{
    int  n, rs ;

    printf ( "Enter number:\n345" ) ;
    scanf ( "%d", &n ) ;
    rs = rsum ( n ) ;
    printf ( "Sum of digits = %d\n", rs ) ;

    return 0 ;
}

int rsum ( int  num )
{
    int  sum, digit ;

    if ( num != 0 )
    {
        digit = num % 10 ;
        num = num / 10 ;
        sum = digit + rsum( num ) ;
    }
    else
        return ( 0 ) ;

    return ( sum ) ;
```

}

## Sample Run

Enter number:
345
Sum of digits = 12

## Explanation

In the **rsum( )** function, we extract the last digit, reduce the number and call **rsum( )** with reduced value of **num**. Thus if the number entered is 3256, the call becomes **s = 6 + rsum ( 325 )**. During each call such additions are kept pending, for example the addition to 6 is kept pending as the program calls **rsum ( 325 )** to obtain sum of digits of 325. These recursive calls end when **n** falls to 0, whereupon the function returns a 0, because sum of digits of 0 is 0. The 0, however is not returned to **main( )**. It is returned to the previous pending call, i.e. **s = 3 + rsum ( 0 )**. Now **s = 3 + 0** is completed and the control reaches **return ( s )**. Now the value of **s**, i.e. 3 is returned to the previous call made during the pending addition **2 + rsum ( 3 )**. This way all pending calls are completed and finally the sum of 3256 is returned to **main( )**.

In short, **return ( 0 )** goes to work only once (during the last call to **rsum( )**), whereas, for all previous calls **return ( s )** goes to work.

## Challenge 48

Write a program that uses recursion to calculate factorial value of a number entered through the keyboard.

Index it

## Solution

```
/* Recursive factorial */
#include <stdio.h>
int refact ( int ) ;

int main( )
{
```

```c
    int  num, fact ;

    printf ( "Enter any number:\n" ) ;
    scanf ( "%d", &num ) ;

    fact = refact ( num ) ;
    printf ( "Factorial value = %d\n", fact ) ;

    return 0 ;
}

int  refact ( int  n )
{
    int  p ;

    if ( n == 0 )
        return ( 1 ) ;
    else
        p = n * refact ( n - 1 ) ;

    return ( p ) ;
}
```

## Sample Run

```
Enter any number
5
Factorial value = 120
```

## Explanation

The explanation is similar to Challenge 47. **return ( 1 )** goes to work only once (during the last call to **refact( )**), whereas, for all previous calls **return ( p )** goes to work. We return 1 when **n** becomes 0 because 0! is equal to 1.

# Challenge 49

Paper of size A0 has dimensions 1189 mm x 841 mm. Each subsequent size A(n) is defined as A(n-1) cut in half parallel to its shorter sides. Write a program to calculate and print paper sizes A0, A1, A2, ... A8 using recursion.

## Solution

```
/* Calculation of PaperSizes A0 to A8 using recursion */
#include <stdio.h>
void papersizes ( int, int, int, int ) ;

int main( )
{
    papersizes ( 0, 7, 1189, 841 ) ;
}

void papersizes ( int i, int n, int l, int b )
{
    int newl, newb ;

    if ( n != 0 )
    {
        printf ( "A%d:L = %d B = %d\n", i, l, b ) ;
        newb = l / 2 ;
        newl = b ;
        n-- ;
        i++ ;
        papersizes ( i, n, newl, newb ) ;
    }
}
```

## Sample Run

```
A0:L = 1189 B = 841
A1:L = 841 B = 594
A2:L = 594 B = 420
```

A3:L = 420 B = 297
A4:L = 297 B = 210
A5:L = 210 B = 148
A6:L = 148 B = 105

## Explanation

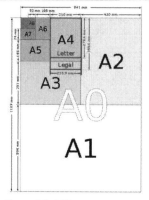

Figure 6.2. *Different paper sizes.*

Figure 6.2 shows how the different paper sizes are obtained. In **papersizes( )**, **i** is used to obtain the digit in A0, A1, A2, etc., whereas **n** is used to keep track of number of times the function should be called. The moment **n** falls to 0, the recursive calls are stopped. Alternately, we could have dropped **n** and stopped recursive calls when **i** reaches 7.

## Challenge 50

Write a recursive function to obtain the first 25 numbers of a Fibonacci sequence. In a Fibonacci sequence the sum of two successive terms gives the third term. Following are the first few terms of the Fibonacci sequence:

1  1  2  3  5  8  13  21  34  55  89....

## Solution

```
/* Generate first 25 terms of a fibonacci sequence using recursion */
# include <stdio.h>
void fibo ( int, int, int ) ;

int main( )
{
    int i, t, old = 1, current = 1 ;

    printf ( "%d\t%d\t", old, current ) ;
    fibo ( old, current, 23 ) ;

    return 0 ;
}

void fibo ( int old, int current, int terms )
{
    int new ;

    if ( terms >= 1 )
    {
        new = old + current ;
        printf ( "%d\t", new ) ;
        terms = terms - 1 ;
        fibo ( current, new, terms ) ;
    }
}
```

## Sample Run

```
1    1    2    3    5    8    13   21   34   55   89   144   233
377  610  987  1597 2584 4181 6765 10946 17711 28657
46368 75025
```

## Explanation

This program generates the Fibonacci sequence of numbers using recursion. **terms** is used to keep track of when to stop recursive calls.

Since the first two terms are printed in **main( )**, we have generated only 23 terms through the recursive calls.

## Challenge 51

A positive integer is entered through the keyboard; write a function to find the binary equivalent of this number using recursion.

### Solution

```c
/* Binary equivalent of a decimal number using recursion */
# include <stdio.h>
int  dec_to_binary ( int  ) ;

int main( )
{
    int  num ;

    printf ( "Enter the number:\n" ) ;
    scanf ( "%d", &num ) ;
    printf ( "The binary equivalent is:\n" ) ;
    dec_to_binary ( num ) ;

    return 0 ;
}

int dec_to_binary ( int  n )
{
    int  r ;

    r = n % 2 ;
    n = n / 2 ;
    if ( n != 0 )
        dec_to_binary ( n ) ;

    printf ( "%d", r ) ;
}
```

## Sample Runs

Enter the number:
32
The binary equivalent is:
100000

Enter the number:
45
The binary equivalent is:
101101

## Explanation

To obtain binary equivalent of a number, we have to keep dividing the dividend till it doesn't become 0. Finally, the remainders obtained during each successive division must be written in reverse order to get the binary equivalent. Since the remainders are to be written in the reverse order, we start printing only when **n** falls to 0, otherwise we make a call to **dec_to_binary( )** with a reduced dividend value.

## Challenge 52

Write a recursive function to obtain the running sum of first 25 natural numbers.

## Solution

```
/* Program to obtain running sum of natural numbers using recursion */
#include <stdio.h>
int runningSum ( int ) ;

int  main( )
{
    int  max, sum ;

    printf ( "Enter the positive largest number for running sum:\n" ) ;
    scanf ( "%d", &max ) ;
```

```
    if ( max > 0 )
    {
        sum = runningSum ( max ) ;
        printf ( "Running Sum: %d\n", sum ) ;
    }
    else
        printf ( "Entered number is negative\n" ) ;

    return 0 ;
}

int  runningSum ( int  n )
{
    int  s ;

    if ( n == 0 )
        return 0 ;
    else
    {
        s = n + runningSum ( n - 1 ) ;
        return ( s ) ;
    }
}
```

## Sample Run

Enter the positive largest number for running sum:
25
Running Sum: 325

## Explanation

We calculate the running sum as we calculate the factorial value,
starting from **n** and then go on reducing it moving towards 0. We stop
on reaching 0.

# 07 / Total Challenges: 5

# Preprocessor Challenges

**W**e can write C programs without knowing anything about the preprocessor, but we should rather not. All good, generalized and maintainable programs usually use C preprocessor directives in them. This chapter presents some preprocessor challenges. If you can solve them you are well on your way to becoming a mature C programmer.

YASHAVANT & ADITYA KANETKAR'S

**101 Challenges**

In C Programming

Solve 101 Challenges to hone C Programming skills
Practise them to be a mature C programmer

## Challenge 53

Write down macro definitions for the following and use them from main( ):

1.  To test whether a character is a small case letter or not.
2.  To test whether a character is an upper case letter or not.
3.  To test whether a character is an alphabet or not. Make use of the macros you defined in 1 and 2 above.
4.  To obtain the bigger of two numbers.

## Solution

```c
# include <stdio.h>

#define ISUPPER(x)    ( x >= 65 && x <= 90 ? 1 : 0 )
#define ISLOWER(x)    ( x >= 97 && x <= 122 ? 1 : 0 )
#define ISALPHA(x)    ( ISUPPER(x) || ISLOWER(x) )
#define MAX(x,y)      ( x > y ? x : y )

int main( )
{
    char ch ;
    int  a, b, big ;

    printf ( "Enter any alphabet/character:\n" ) ;
    scanf ( "%c", &ch ) ;

    if ( ISUPPER ( ch ) )
        printf ( "You entered a capital letter\n" ) ;

    if ( ISLOWER ( ch ) )
        printf ( "You entered a small case letter\n" ) ;

    if ( ISALPHA ( ch ) )
        printf ( "You entered an alphabet\n" ) ;

    printf ( "Enter any two numbers:\n" ) ;
    scanf ( "%d%d", &a, &b ) ;
```

```
    printf ( "Bigger number is %d\n", MAX ( a,b ) ) ;

    return 0 ;
}
```

## Sample Run

```
Enter any character:
A
You entered a capital letter
You entered an alphabet
Enter any two numbers:
45 66
Bigger number is 66
```

## Explanation

During preprocessing the statement **if ( ISUPPER ( ch ) )** gets replaced by **if ( ch >= 65 && ch <= 90 ? 1 : 0 )**. Same goes for other macros. Note that while defining one macro, other macros can be used. For example, for defining **ISALPHA** macro, the macros **ISUPPER** and **ISLOWER** are being used. Also note that a macro can take multiple arguments, like the **MAX** macro in our program.

## Challenge 54

Write macro definitions with arguments for calculation of area and perimeter of a triangle, a square and a circle. Store these macro definitions in a file called "areaperi.h". Include this file in your program, and call the macro definitions for calculating area and perimeter for a square, triangle and circle.

## Solution

```
/* areaperi.h */

#define PI 3.1428
#define AREAC( r )      ( PI * r * r )
```

```
#define PERIC( r )      ( 2 * PI * r )
#define AREAS( x )      ( x * x )
#define PERIS( x )      ( 4 * x )
#define PERIT( x, y, z )  ( x + y + z )
#define SPERI( a, b, c ) ( ( a + b + c ) / 2 )
#define AREAT( a, b, c )   sqrt( SPERI( a, b, c ) * \
                           ( SPERI( a, b, c ) - a ) * \
                           ( SPERI( a, b, c ) - b ) * \
                           ( SPERI( a, b, c ) - c ) )
```

*Area of triangle uung Heron's formula* a

*Using backslash when definition spread over multiple lines*

```
/* Program that use macros in header file areaperi.h */

# include <stdio.h>
# include <math.h>
#include "areaperi.h"

int main( )
{
    float  r, p_cir, a_cir ;
    float  sid, p_sqr, a_sqr ;
    float  sid1, sid2, sid3, a_tri, p_tri ;

    printf ( "Enter radius of circle:\n" ) ;
    scanf ( "%f", &r ) ;
    a_cir = AREAC ( r ) ;
    printf ( "Area of circle = %f\n", a_cir ) ;
    p_cir = PERIC ( r ) ;
    printf ( "Circumference of circle = %f\n", p_cir ) ;

    printf ( "Enter side of a square:\n" ) ;
    scanf ( "%f", &sid ) ;
    a_sqr = AREAS ( sid ) ;
    printf ( "Area of square = %f\n", a_sqr ) ;
    p_sqr = PERIS ( sid ) ;
    printf ( "Perimeter of square = %f\n", p_sqr ) ;

    printf ( "Enter length of 3 sides of triangle:\n" ) ;
    scanf ( "%f %f %f", &sid1, &sid2, &sid3 ) ;
    a_tri = AREAT ( sid1, sid2, sid3 ) ;
    printf ( "Area of triangle = %f\n", a_tri ) ;
```

```
p_tri = PERIT ( sid1, sid2, sid3 ) ;
printf ( "Perimeter of triangle = %f\n", p_tri ) ;

return 0 ;
}
```

## Sample Run

```
Enter radius of circle:
1
Area of circle = 3.141500
Circumference of circle = 6.283000
Enter side of a square:
5
Area of square = 25.000000
Perimeter of square = 20.000000
Enter length of 3 sides of triangle:
3 4 5
Area of triangle = 6.000000
Perimeter of triangle = 12.000000
```

## Explanation

It is agood idea to use the macro PI instead of straight-away using the value 3.1428. This ensures that the same value is available consistenly throughout the program. This becomes especially useful if we were to use the value of pi at several places in the program.

The macros written in "areaperi.h" get imported and get placed on top of **main( )** at the place where the file is #included.

Note the usage of " " instead of < > while including areaperi.h. " " ensure that file would be searched by the preprocessor in the current project's directory apart from the standard include path.

## Challenge 55

Write down macro definitions for the following:

1. To find arithmetic mean of two numbers.
2. To find absolute value of a number.

3. To convert an uppercase alphabet to lowercase.
4. To obtain the biggest of three numbers.

## Solution

```c
# include <stdio.h>

#define MEAN(x,y)    ( ( x + y ) / 2 )
#define ABS(x)       ( x < 0 ? x * - 1 : x )
#define TOLOWER(x)   ( x + 32 )
#define MAX(x,y,z)   ( x > y && x > z ? x : y > x && y > z ? y : z )

int main( )
{
    int  a, b, c, m, val, big ;
    char  ch ;

    printf ( "Enter any two numbers:\n" ) ;
    scanf ( "%d %d", &a, &b ) ;

    m = MEAN ( a, b ) ;  /* Macro substitution */
    printf ( "Mean is %d\n", m ) ;

    printf ( "Enter any number:\n" ) ;
    scanf ( "%d", &a ) ;

    val = ABS ( a ) ;
    printf ( "Absolute value is %d\n", val ) ;

    fflush ( stdin ) ;
    printf ( "Enter any upper case character:\n" ) ;
    scanf ( "%c", &ch ) ;

    ch = TOLOWER ( ch ) ;
    printf ( "Lower case character is %c\n", ch ) ;

    printf ( "Enter any three numbers:\n" ) ;
    scanf ( "%d %d %d", &a, &b, &c ) ;

    big = MAX ( a, b, c ) ;
    printf ( "Biggest number is: %d\n", big ) ;
```

*alternatively getchar() can also be used.*

*This consumes the new line character before the character is saved to "ch" variable*

```
    return 0 ;
}
```

## Sample Run

```
Enter any two numbers:
12 34
Mean is 23
Enter any number:
-4
Absolute value is 4
Enter any upper case character:
Z
Lower case character is z
Enter any three numbers:
12 12 23
Biggest number is: 23
```

## Explanation

Refer explanation of challenge 54.

## Challenge 56

Write macro definitions with arguments for calculation of Simple Interest and Amount. Store these macro definitions in a file called "interest.h". Include this file in your program, and use the macro definitions for calculating simple interest and amount.

## Solution

```
/* interest.h */
#define SI( p, n, r ) ( p * n * r / 100 )
#define AMT( p, si ) ( p + si )


/* interest.c */
# include <stdio.h>
```

```c
# include "interest.h"

int main( )
{
    int  p, n ;
    float  si, amt, r ;

    printf ( "Enter Principal, no. of years and rate of interest:\n" ) ;
    scanf ( "%d %d %f", &p, &n, &r ) ;

    si = SI ( p, n, r ) ;
    amt = AMT ( p, si ) ;

    printf ( "Simple interest is: %f\n", si ) ;
    printf ( "Amount is: %f\n", amt ) ;

    return 0 ;
}
```

## Sample Run

```
Enter Principal, no. of years and rate of interest:
1000 3 15.5
Simple interest is: 465.000000
Amount is: 1465.000000
```

## Explanation

Refer explanation of challenge 54.

## ✓ Challenge 57

Write macro definitions for the following and use them in main( ):

DEGREES - Converts radians into degrees
RADIANS - Converts degrees into radians
ODD - Rounds a number up to the nearest odd integer
EVEN - Rounds a number up to the nearest even integer

## Solution

```
# include <stdio.h>

#define PI 3.14
#define RAD( a ) ( a * PI / 180 )
#define DEG( n ) ( n * 180 / PI )
#define ODD( n ) ( n % 2 == 0 ? n + 1 : n )
#define EVEN( n ) ( n % 2 == 1 ? n + 1 : n )

int main( )
{
    float  deg, rad ;
    int  num, odd, even ;

    printf ( "Enter an angle in degrees:\n" ) ;
    scanf ( "%f", &deg ) ;
    rad = RAD( deg ) ;
    printf ( "deg = %f rad = %f\n", deg, rad ) ;

    deg = DEG( rad ) ;
    printf ( "rad = %f deg = %f\n", rad, deg ) ;

    printf ( "Enter a number:\n" ) ;
    scanf ( "%d", &num ) ;
    odd = ODD ( num ) ;
    printf ( "num = %d nearerst odd = %d\n", num, odd ) ;

    printf ( "Enter a number:\n" ) ;
    scanf ( "%d", &num ) ;
    even = EVEN ( num ) ;
    printf ( "num = %d nearerst even = %d\n", num, even ) ;

    return 0 ;
}
```

## Sample Run

```
Enter an angle in degrees:
90
```

```
deg = 90.000000 rad = 1.570000
rad = 1.570000 deg = 90.000000
Enter a number:
35
num = 35 nearerst odd = 35
Enter a number:
23
num = 23 nearerst even = 24
```

## Explanation

Refer explanation of challenge 54.

# 08 / Total Challenges: 11

# Array Challenges

Ordinary variables are capable of holding only one value at a time. If there is a large amount of similar data to be handled, then using a different variable for each data item would make the job unwieldy, tedious and confusing. Instead, on combining all this similar data into an array, the whole task of organizing and manipulating data would become easier and more efficient. This chapter presents challenges that need arrays to conquer.

## Challenge 58

If 25 numbers are entered through the keyboard, write a program to calculate their mean, median and mode values.

### Solution

```
/* Calculate mean, median, mode of a set of numbers */
#include <stdio.h>
#define MAX 25

int main( )
{
    int  mean, median, mode, freq, newmode, newfreq ;
    int  arr[ MAX ] ;
    int  i, j, k, t, sum  ;

    printf ( "Enter %d numbers:\n", MAX ) ;
    for ( i = 0 ; i < MAX ; i++ )
        scanf ( "%d", &arr[ i ] ) ;

    sum = 0 ;
    for ( i = 0 ; i < MAX ; i++ )
        sum = sum + arr[ i ] ;

    mean = sum / MAX ;

    /* sort numbers */
    for ( i = 0 ; i < MAX ; i++ )
    {
        for ( j = i + 1 ; j < MAX ; j++ )
        {
            if ( arr[ i ] > arr[ j ] )
            {
                t = arr[ i ] ;
                arr[ i ] = arr[ j ] ;
                arr[ j ] = t ;
            }
        }
```

```
    }

    if ( MAX % 2 == 0 )
        median = ( arr[ MAX / 2 - 1 ] + arr[ MAX / 2 ] ) / 2 ;
    else
        median = arr[ ( MAX - 1 ) / 2 ] ;

    mode = arr[ 0 ] ;
    freq = 1 ;
    k = 0 ;
    for ( i = 0 ; i < MAX ; )
    {
        newmode = arr[ k ] ;
        newfreq = 1 ;
        for ( j = i + 1 ; j < MAX ; j++ )
        {
            if ( arr[ i ] == arr[ j ] )
                newfreq++ ;
            else
                break ;
        }

        if ( newfreq >= freq )
        {
            mode = newmode ;
            freq = newfreq ;
        }
        i = k = j ;
    }

    printf ( "Mean = %d\n", mean ) ;
    printf ( "Median = %d\n", median ) ;
    printf ( "Mode = %d\n", mode ) ;

    return 0 ;
}
```

// If current freq is greter than previous freancy

## Sample Run

Enter 25 numbers:

12 12 12 12 12 13 13 13 14 15 15 15 15 15 15 15 15 15 16 16 16 17 17
17 17
Mean = 14
Median = 15
Mode = 15

## Explanation

Calculation of mean is simple. Through a **for** loop we calculate the
running sum of all 25 numbers stored in the array **arr[ ]**. Then we divide
it by 25 to obtain the mean. Note the usage of **MAX** instead of 25. This
would make the program generic. Tomorrow if we have to obtain the
mean of 30 numbers, we simply have to replace 25 with 30 in definition
of **MAX**, rest would be taken care of.

To obtain median we first sort numbers in ascending order using the
Bubble Sort logic implemented through a pair of **for** loops. Next,
depending upon whether **arr[ ]** has odd or even entries we obtain the
median as either the middle value or the average of the two middle
values.

Obtaining mode is the most difficult part in this challenge. To obtain this
we have to begin with an assumtion that the very first number is the
mode value. Then we iterate through the array counting how many
times each number occurs in it. Each time we obtain a number with a
higher frequency we note its value in **mode** and its frequency in **freq**.
The final value in **mode** is the result that we desire.

## Challenge 59

Write a program to implement a stack data structure. Stack is a LIFO
(Last In First Out) list in which addition and deletion takes place at the
same end.

## Solution

```
#include <stdio.h>
#define MAX 10
#define TRUE 1
#define FALSE 0
```

```
void push ( int ) ;
int pop( ) ;
```

— } Function Prototypes

```
int  arr[ MAX ] ;
int  top ;
int  empty = TRUE ;

int main( )
{
    int  n ;

    top = -1 ;
    push ( 11 ) ;
    push ( 23 ) ;
    push ( -8 ) ;
    push ( 14 ) ;
    push ( 20 ) ;
    push ( 21 ) ;
    push ( 2 ) ;
    push ( -3 ) ;
    push ( 4 ) ;
    push ( 12 ) ;
    push ( 5 ) ;
```

— Initially the Stack is empty

```
    n = pop( ) ;
    if ( n == -1 && empty == TRUE )
        printf ( "Stack is empty. Cannot pop\n" ) ;
    else
        printf ( "Popped Element: %d\n", n ) ;

    n = pop( ) ;
    if ( n == -1 && empty == TRUE )
        printf ( "Stack is empty. Cannot pop\n" ) ;
    else
        printf ( "Popped Element: %d\n", n ) ;

    n = pop( ) ;
    if ( n == -1 && empty == TRUE )
        printf ( "Stack is empty. Cannot pop\n" ) ;
    else
```

```
        printf ( "Popped Element: %d\n", n ) ;

    return 0 ;
}

void push ( int num )
{
    if ( top == MAX - 1 )
    {
        printf ( "Stack is full. Cannot push element\n" ) ;
        return ;
    }

    top++ ;
    arr[ top ] = num ;
    empty = FALSE ;
}

int pop( )
{
    int num ;

    if ( top == -1 )
    {
        empty = TRUE ;
        return -1 ;
    }

    num = arr[ top ] ;
    top-- ;

    return num ;
}
```

*To add a element to a stack*

*TO remove a element from stack*

→ *Return -1 if the stack is empty*

## Sample Run

```
Stack is full.
Item popped: 12
Item popped: 4
Item popped: -3
Item popped: 2
```

## Explanation

While performing a push operation number is added to the array **arr[ ]**, whereas, while performing a pop operation a number would be removed from **arr[ ]** (the element is not physically removed from the array though). Both these addition and deletion happen at an index into the array, being maintained using the variable **top**.

Since the array elements are counted from 0 onwards, to begin with when the stack is empty, **top** is set to -1 and **empty** is set to TRUE to indicate emptyness of stack. During each push operation firstly **top** is incremented and the then the element being pushed is stored at **arr[ top ]**. Since we are storing an element in stack, **empty** is set to FALSE. If **top** reaches **MAX -1** it means there is no space left in the array to accommodate any more elements. This is then reported as stack is full.

During popping, exactly reverse operations are done. Firsly the number at **arr[ top ]** is collected in **data** and then value of **top** is reduced by 1. Here too, care is taken to check whether **top** has fallen to -1. If so, without popping an element **empty** is set to TRUE and it is appropriately reported that the stack is empty.

Note that **top** and **empty** are declared as global variables because they are required by all three functions in the program.

*[handwritten margin note: Max - 1 indicates that the stack is full]*

## Challenge 60

Twenty-five numbers are entered from the keyboard into an array. Write a program to find the number of positives, negatives and zeros in the array.

## Solution

```c
/* Calculate frequency of positives, negatives, zeros */
#include <stdio.h>
#define MAX 25

int main( )
{
    int  num[ MAX ] ;
```

```
int  i, pos, zeros, neg ;

printf ( "Enter 25 elements of array:\n" ) ;
for ( i = 0 ; i < MAX ; i++ )
    scanf ( "%d", &num[ i ] ) ; /* Array Elements */

pos = zeros = neg = 0;
for ( i = 0 ; i <= 24 ; i++ )
{
    if ( num[ i ] > 0 )
        pos++ ;
    else if ( num[ i ] == 0 )
        zeros++ ;
    else
        neg++ ;
}

printf ( "Number of positives = %d\n", pos ) ;
printf ( "Number of negatives = %d\n", neg ) ;
printf ( "Number of zeros = %d\n", zeros ) ;

return 0 ;
}
```

## Sample Run

```
Enter 25 elements of array:
1 2 3 4 5 3 3 3 3 3 6 6 6 6 6 -3 4 5 -6 -7 0 0 0 -5 0
Number of positives = 17
Number of negatives = 4
Number of zeros = 4
```

## Explanation

This challenge is fairly straight-forward. Through a **for** loop we keep running sums of positives, negatives and zeros present in the array.

## Challenge 61

 *Index it*         *Quick Sort*

Write a program to implement the Quick Sort algorithm on an array of 10 integers.

### Solution

```c
/* Sort numbers using Quick Sort algorithm */
#include <stdio.h>
                        Pointer to an Int
void quicksort ( int *, int, int ) ;
int split ( int *, int, int ) ;

int main( )         Pointer to an Int
{
    int arr[10] = { 11, 2, 9, 13, 57, 25, 17, 1, 90, 3 } ;
    int i ;

    printf ( "Array before sorting:\n") ;     Prints array before
                                                        Sorting
    for ( i = 0 ; i <= 9 ; i++ )
        printf ( "%d\t", arr[ i ] ) ;

    quicksort ( arr, 0, 9 ) ;

    printf ( "\n" ) ;
    printf ( "Array after sorting:\n") ;      Prints array after
                                                        Sorting
    for ( i = 0 ; i <= 9 ; i++ )
        printf ( "%d\t", arr[ i ] ) ;

    return 0 ;
}

void quicksort ( int  *a, int  lower, int  upper )
{
    int  i ;

    if ( upper > lower )
```

```
    {
        i = split ( a, lower, upper ) ;
        quicksort ( a, lower, i - 1 ) ;
        quicksort ( a, i + 1, upper ) ;
    }
}

int split ( int  *a, int  lower, int  upper )
{
    int  i, p, q, t ;

    p = lower + 1 ;
    q = upper ;
    i = a[ lower ] ;        — First array element

    while ( q >= p )
    {
        while ( a[ p ] < i )
            p++ ;

        while ( a[ q ] > i )
            q-- ;

        if ( q > p )            Replace the higher
        {                       element at P with
            t = a[ p ] ;        the lower element
            a[ p ] = a[ q ] ;           at q
            a[ q ] = t ;
        }
    }

    t = a[ lower ] ;
    a[ lower ] = a[ q ] ;
    a[ q ] = t ;

    return q ;
}
```

## Sample Run

Array before sorting:
11   2   9   13   57   25   17   1   90   3
Array after sorting:
1   2   3   9   11   13   17   25   57   90

## Explanation

Quick sort is a very popular sorting method. The name comes from the fact that, in general, quick sort can sort a list of data elements significantly faster than any of the common sorting algorithms. This algorithm is based on the fact that it is faster and easier to sort two small arrays than one larger array. Thus, the basic strategy of quick sort is to divide and conquer.

If you were given a large stack of papers bearing the names of the students to sort them by name, you might use the following approach. Pick a splitting value, say L (known as **pivot** element) and divide the stack of papers into two piles, A-L and M-Z (note that the two piles will not necessarily contain the same number of papers). Then take the first pile and sub-divide it into two piles, A-F and G-L. The A-F pile can be further broken down into A-C and D-F. This division process goes on until the piles are small enough to be easily sorted. The same process is applied to the M-Z pile. Eventually all the small sorted piles can be stacked one on top of the other to produce an ordered set of papers.

This strategy is based on recursion—on each attempt to sort the stack of papers the pile is divided and then the same approach is used to sort each smaller piles (a smaller case).

Quick sort is also known as **partition exchange sort.** The quick sort procedure can be explained with the help of Figure 8.1. In Figure 8.1 the element that is indicated by '*' is the pivot element and the element that is indicated by '—' is the element whose position is finalized.

Quick Sort uses the divide & conquer approach

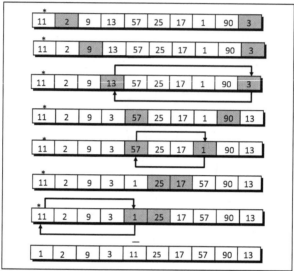

Figure 8.1. *Quick sort.*

Suppose an array **arr** consists of **10** distinct elements. The quick sort algorithm works as follows:

(a) In the first iteration, we will place the $0^{th}$ element 11 at its final position and divide the array. Here, 11 is the pivot element. To divide the array, two index variables, **p** and **q**, are taken. The indexes are initialized in such a way that, **p** refers to the $1^{st}$ element 2 and **q** refers to the $(n - 1)^{th}$ element 3.

(b) The job of index variable **p** is to search an element that is greater than the value at $0^{th}$ location. So **p** is incremented by one till the value stored at **p** is greater than $0^{th}$ element. In our case it is incremented till 13, as 13 is greater that 11.

(c) Similarly, **q** needs to search an element that is smaller than the $0^{th}$ element. So **q** is decremented by one till the value stored at **q** is smaller than the value at $0^{th}$ location. In our case **q** is not decremented because 3 is less than 11.

(d) When these elements are found they are interchanged. Again from the current positions **p** and **q** are incremented and decremented respectively and exchanges are made appropriately if desired.

(e) The process ends whenever the index pointers meet or crossover. In our case, they cross at the values 1 and 25 for the indexes **q** and **p** respectively. Finally, the $0^{th}$ element 11 is interchanged with the value at index **q**, i.e. 1. The position **q** is now the final position of the pivot element 11.

(f) As a result, the whole array is divided into two parts, such that all the elements before 11 are less than 11 and all the elements after 11 are greater than 11.

(g) Now the same procedure is applied for the two sub-arrays. As a result, at the end when all sub-arrays are left with one element, the original array becomes sorted.

Here, it is not necessary that the pivot element whose position is to be finalized in the first iteration must be the $0^{th}$ element. It can be any other element as well.

The arguments being passed to the function **quicksort( )** would reflect the part of the array that is being currently processed. We will pass the first and last indexes that define the part of the array to be processed during this call. The initial call to **quicksort( )** would contain the arguments 0 and 9, since there are 10 integers in our array.

In the function **quicksort( )**, a condition is checked whether **upper** is greater than **lower**. If the condition is satisfied then only the array will be split into two parts, otherwise, the control will simply be returned. To split the array into two parts the function **split( )** is called.

In the function **split( )**, to start with the two variables **p** and **q** are taken which are assigned with the values **lower + 1** and **upper**. Then a **while** loop is executed that checks whether the indices **p** and **q** have crossed each other. If they have not crossed, then inside the **while** loop two more nested **while** loops are executed to increase the index **p** and decrease the index **q** to their appropriate places. Then it is checked whether **q** is greater than **p**. If so, then the elements present at $p^{th}$ and $q^{th}$ positions are interchanged.

Finally, when the control returns to the function **quicksort( )** two recursive calls are made to function **quicksort( )**. This is done to sort the two split sub-arrays. As a result, after all the recursive calls when the control reaches the function **main( )** the array stands sorted.

## Challenge 62

Write a program to perfrom a Linear Search on an array of 10 integers.

## Solution

```
/* Linear Search in an array */
#include <stdio.h>
int main( )
{
    int  arr[ 10 ] = { 11, 2, 9, 13, 57, 25, 17, 1, 90, 3 } ;
    int  i, num ;

    printf ( "Enter number to search:\n" ) ;
    scanf ( "%d", &num ) ;

    for ( i = 0 ; i <= 9 ; i++ )
    {
        if ( arr[ i ] == num )
            break ;
    }

    if ( i == 10 )
        printf ( "Number is not present in the array\n" ) ;
    else
        printf ( "The number is at position %d in the array\n", i ) ;

    return 0 ;
}
```

## Sample Run

Enter number to search: 57
The number is at position 4 in the array

## Explanation

This is the simplest method of searching. In this method, the element is sequentially searched in the list. This method can be applied to a sorted or an unsorted list. Searching is case of a sorted list starts from 0th element and continues until the element is found or an element whose value is greater (assuming the list is sorted in ascending order) than the value being searched is reached. As against this, searching in case of unsorted list starts from the 0th element and continues until the element is found or the end of list is reached.

Let us now try to understand this with the help of example. Consider the array shown in Figure 8.2.

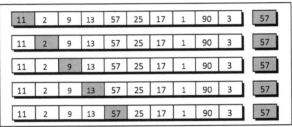

Figure 8.2. *Linear search in an unsorted array.*

The array shown in figure consists of 10 numbers. Suppose the element that is to be searched is 57. So 57 is compared with all the elements starting with 0th element and the searching process ends either when 57 is found or the list ends.

In the program, **num** is the number that is to be searched in the array **arr**. Inside the **for** loop each time **arr[ i ]** is compared with **num**. If any element is equal to **num** then that's the position of element where the number being searched is found. Hence **break** is applied to the **for** loop.

This method can be applied to a sored or unsorted list

Index it →

Binary Search

## Challenge 63

Write a program to perfrom a Binary Search on an array of 10 integers.

## Solution

```c
#include <stdio.h>
#define MAX 10
#define FOUND 1
#define NOTFOUND 0

int main( )
{
    int arr[ MAX ] = { 1, 2, 3, 9, 11, 13, 17, 25, 57, 90 } ;
    int mid, lower, upper, num, flag ;

    lower = 0 ;
    upper = MAX - 1 ;
    flag = NOTFOUND ;

    printf ( "Enter number to search:\n" ) ;
    scanf ( "%d", &num ) ;

    mid = ( lower + upper ) / 2 ;
    while ( lower <= upper )
    {
        if ( arr[ mid ] == num )
        {
            printf ( "Number is at position %d in the array\n",  mid ) ;
            flag = FOUND ;
            break ;
        }

        if ( arr[ mid ] > num )
            upper = mid - 1 ;
        else
            lower = mid + 1 ;

        mid = ( lower + upper ) / 2 ;
```

Keep Splitting the array
in the middle &
then check if the
"Search element" lie in
the lower half / upper half

```
    }

    if ( flag == NOTFOUND )
        printf ( "Element is not present in the array\n" ) ;

    return 0 ;
}
```

## Sample Run

Enter number to search: 57
The number is at position 8 in the array

## Explanation

Binary search method is very fast and efficient. This method requires that the list of elements be in sorted order.

In this method, to search an element we compare it with the element present at the center of the list. If it matches then the search is successful. Otherwise, the list is divided into two halves: one from $0^{th}$ element to the center element (first half), and another from center element to the last element (second half). As a result, all the elements in first half are smaller than the center element, whereas, all the elements in second half are greater than the center element.

The searching will now proceed in either of the two halves depending upon whether the element is greater or smaller than the center element. If the element is smaller than the center element then the searching will be done in the first half, otherwise in the second half.

Same process of comparing the required element with the center element, and if not found then dividing the elements into two halves is repeated for the first half or second half. This procedure is repeated till the element is found or the division of half parts gives one element. Let us understand this with the help of Figure 8.3.

*[Handwritten margin notes: Search for the element at the exact Middle. – If not found – Split from first element to Middle – From middle to last element. This method require that the array be sorted first]*

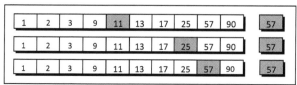

Figure 8.3. *Binary search.*

Suppose an array **arr** consists of 10 sorted numbers and 57 is element that is to be searched. The binary search method when applied to this array works as follows:

(a) 57 is compared with the element present at the center of the list (i.e. 11). Since 57 is greater than 11, the searching is restricted only to the second half of the array.

(b) Now 57 is compared with the center element of the second half of array (i.e. 25). Here again 57 is greater than 25 so the searching now proceeds in the elements present between the 25 and the last element 90.

(c) This process is repeated till 57 is found or no further division of sub-array is possible.

In the program each time through the loop **arr[ mid ]** is compared with **num** as **mid** holds the index of the middle element of array. If **num** is found then the search ends. If it is not found, then for further searching it is checked whether **num** is present in lower half or upper half of the array. If **num** is found to be smaller than the middle element then **mid − 1** is made the upper limit, keeping lower limit as it is. Otherwise **mid + 1** is made the lower limit of searching, keeping the upper limit as it is. During each iteration the value of **mid** is calculated, as **mid = ( lower + upper ) / 2**.

## Challenge 64

Write a program to check whether the contents of two 1D arrays are same or not.

## Solution

/* Check whether two arrays are equal or not */

```
#include <stdio.h>
#define EQUAL 1
#define NOTEQUAL 0

int compare ( int*, int, int*, int ) ;

int main ( )
{
    int  arr1[ ] = { 1, 2, 3, 4, 5 };
    int  arr2[ ] = { 2, 3, 4, 5, 6 };
    int  arr3[ ] = { 2, 4, 6, 8 };
    int  arr4[ ] = { 1, 2, 3, 4, 5 };

    int  result ;

    result = compare ( arr1, 5, arr2, 5 ) ;
    if ( result == EQUAL )
        printf ( "Arrays arr1 and arr2 are equal\n" ) ;
    else
        printf ( "Arrays arr1 and arr2 are not equal\n" ) ;

    result = compare ( arr1, 5, arr3, 4 ) ;
    if ( result == EQUAL )
        printf ( "Arrays arr1 and arr3 are equal\n" ) ;
    else
        printf ( "Arrays arr1 and arr3 are not equal\n" ) ;

    result = compare ( arr1, 5, arr4, 5 ) ;
    if ( result == EQUAL )
        printf ( "Arrays arr1 and arr4 are equal\n" ) ;
    else
        printf ( "Arrays arr1 and arr4 are not equal\n" ) ;

    result = compare ( arr2, 5, arr3, 4 ) ;
    if ( result == EQUAL )
        printf ( "Arrays arr2 and arr3 are equal\n" ) ;
    else
        printf ( "Arrays arr2 and arr3 are not equal\n" ) ;
}

int compare ( int  *arr1, int  sz1, int  *arr2, int  sz2 )
```

*Handwritten annotations:*
- *arr1 and arr2 — Same length*
- *arr3 and arr4 — unequal length*
- *Result not equal*
- *Result not equal*
- *Result equal*
- *Result not equal*

```
{
    int i ;

    if ( sz1 != sz2 )          // If arrays are
        return NOTEQUAL ;          of different size
    else
    {
        for ( i = 0 ; i < sz1 ; i++ )
        {
            if ( arr1[ i ] != arr2[ i ] )    // At the first instance
                return NOTEQUAL ;                of discrepancy
        }

        return EQUAL ;
    }
}
```

## Sample Run

Arrays arr1 and arr2 are not equal
Arrays arr1 and arr3 are not equal
Arrays arr1 and arr4 are equal
Arrays arr2 and arr3 are not equal

## Explanation

In the **compare( )** function, we first check whether the number of elements in the two arrays are same or not. If they are not, without comparing the elements we report that the two arrays are unequal. If the number of elements is equal, then we check the contents of the two arrays element by element. Any time there is a mismatch we stop any further comparisons and report that the two arrays are unequal. If all elements match, we report that the two arrays are equal.

 Index it ✓

## Challenge 65

Write a program that rotates the contents of a 1D array of integers by desired number of places.

## Solution

```
/* Rotate elements of 1D array */
#include <stdio.h>
void printarray ( int*, int ) ;
void rotatearray ( int*, int, int ) ;

int main( )
{
    int  arr[ ] = { 1, 2, 3, 4, 5, 6, 7, 8, 9, 10 } ;

    printarray ( arr, 10 ) ;
    rotatearray ( arr, 10, 10 ) ;
    printarray ( arr, 10 ) ;
}

void printarray ( int*  arr, int  size )
{
    int  i ;

    for ( i = 0 ; i < size ; i++ )
        printf ( "%d\t", arr[ i ] ) ;
    printf ( "\n" ) ;
}

void rotatearray ( int *arr, int  size, int  k )
{
    void rotatearraybyone ( int*, int ) ;
    int i ;

    for ( i = 0; i < k ; i++ )
        rotatearraybyone ( arr, size ) ;
}

void rotatearraybyone ( int *arr, int  n )
{
    int i, tmp ;

    tmp = arr[ 0 ] ;
    for ( i = 0 ; i < n ; i++ )
```

Its a loop which Simply iterate 3 times

Size of array

First Left Rotate

```
        arr[ i ] = arr[ i + 1 ] ;
    arr[ i - 1 ] = tmp ;
}
```

## Sample Run

```
1   2   3   4   5   6   7   8   9   10
1   2   3   4   5   6   7   8   9   10
```

## Explanation

As the name suggests, **rotatearraybyone( )** function rotates all array elements by one position. We have called it from **rotatearray( )** function **k** times.

Note that we have not declared the prototype of **rotatearraybyone( )** on top of **main( )**. This is because we want **rotatearraybyone( )** to be callable only from **rotatearray( )** and not from any other function.

## Challenge 66

*Index it*

Write a program to reverse the contents of a 1D array.

## Solution

```c
/* Reverse the contents of a 1D array */
#include <stdio.h>
void reverse ( int*, int ) ;

int main ( )
{
    int arr[ ] = { 1, 2, 3, 4, 5, 6, 7, 8, 9, 10 } ;
    int i ;

    reverse ( arr, 10 ) ;
    for ( i = 0 ; i < 10 ; i++ )
        printf ( "%d\t", arr[ i ] ) ;
}
```

```c
void reverse ( int *arr, int size )
{
    int  begin, end, t ;

    begin = 0 ;
    end = size - 1 ;

    while ( begin <= end )
    {
        t = arr[ begin ] ;
        arr[ begin ] = arr[ end ] ;
        arr[ end ] = t ;

        begin++ ;
        end-- ;
    }
}
```

## Sample Run

10   9   8   7   6   5   4   3   2   1

## Explanation

The **reverse( )** function excanges first element with last element, second element with second last element, etc. It continues this till **begin** doesn't cross **end.**

## Challenge 67

Write a program to obtain binary equivalent of a positive decimal integer.

## Solution

/* Obtain binary equivalent of a positive integer */

```c
#include <stdio.h>
#include <string.h>
```

*Index it*

```
void binaryEquivalent ( int ) ;
int isValid ( int ) ;

int main( )
{
    int  num ;

    printf ( "Enter a non-negative decimal number\n" ) ;
    scanf ( "%d", &num ) ;

    if ( isValid ( num ) )
        binaryEquivalent ( num ) ;
    else
        printf ( "Invalid input\n" ) ;

    return 0 ;
}

int isValid ( int  n )
{
    if ( n <= 0 )
        return 0 ;
    else
        return 1 ;
}

void binaryEquivalent ( int  n )
{
    char binary[ 100 ] ;  // array of 100 char
    int rem, front, back, index ;
    char ch ;

    index = 0 ;

    while ( n != 0 )
    {
        rem = n % 2 ;
        if ( rem == 0 )
            binary[ index ] = '0' ;
        else
```

```
        binary[ index ] = '1' ;

    index++ ;
    n = n / 2 ;
}
binary[ index ] = '\0' ;

front = 0 ;
back = index - 1 ;

while ( front < back )
{
    ch = binary[ front ] ;
    binary[ front ] = binary[ back ] ;
    binary[ back ] = ch ;

    front++ ;
    back-- ;
}

    printf ( "Binary Equivalent: %s\n", binary ) ;
}
```

*divides the number & saves the remainder 0 or 1 in an array of char*

*Set the last element as a null character*

*Same code as reversal of array elements*

*%s format specifier to print  contents of a char array*

## Sample Run

Enter a non-negative decimal number:
55
Binary Equivalent: 110111

## Explanation

**isValid( )** checks whether the number is positive or not. In the **binaryEquivalent( )** function as we perform successive divisions by 2, we do not print the remainders. Instead, we collect them in a character array called **binay[ ]**. This is necessary because in the binary equivalent of a decimal number, remainders obtained have to be arranged in reverse order. Once the dividend becomes zero, we exchange the contents of the array **binary[ ]** in the following manner:

first with last,
second with last but one,

third with last but two,
etc.

After these exchanges, final contents of the **binary[ ]** array are printed
out.

## Challenge 68

Implement in a program the following procedure to generate prime
numbers from 1 to 100. This procedure is called sieve of Eratosthenes.

Step 1 Fill an array **num[ 100 ]** with numbers from 1 to 100.

Step 2 Starting with the second entry in the array, set all its
multiples to zero.

Step 3 Proceed to the next non-zero element and set all its
multiples to zero.

Step 4 Repeat Step 3 till you have set up the multiples of all the
non-zero elements to zero.

Step 5 At the conclusion of Step 4, all the non-zero entries left in
the array would be prime numbers, so print out these
numbers.

## Solution

```
/* Sieve of Eratosthenes */
# include <stdio.h>
int main( )
{
    int  num[ 100 ], i, j, k, step ;

    /* fill array with numbers from 1 to 100 */
    for ( i = 0 ; i <= 99 ; i++ )
        num[ i ] = i + 1 ;

    for ( i = 1 ; i <= 99 ; i++ )
    {
        if ( num[ i ] != 0 )
        {
            k = num[ i ] * 2 - 1 ;
            step = num[ i ] ;
```

```
        for ( j = k ; j <= 99 ; j = j + step )
            num[ j ] = 0 ;
    }
}

printf ( "\nPrime numbers between 1 & 100 are:\n" ) ;
for ( i = 0 ; i <= 99 ; i++ )
{
    if ( num[ i ] != 0 )
        printf ( "%d\t", num[ i ] ) ;
}

return 0 ;
}
```

## Sample Run

Prime numbers between 1 & 100 are:

| 1 | 2 | 3 | 5 | 7 | 11 | 13 | 17 | 19 | 23 | 29 | 31 | 37 |
|---|---|---|---|---|----|----|----|----|----|----|----|----|
| 41 | 43 | 47 | 53 | 59 | 61 | 67 | 71 | 73 | 79 | 83 | 89 | 97 |

## Explanation

The first **for** loop fills the array **arr[ ]** with numbers from 1 to 100. The second **for** loop visits each array element starting from **arr[ 1 ]** and if it is found to be non-zero then sets all its multiples to 0 through the third **for** loop. The last **for** loop prints all the non-zero elements left in the array, which are indeed the prime numbers.

# 09 / Total Challenges: 5

# Multidimensional Array Challenges

To deal with a set of numbers an array datatype is used and to deal with multiple sets of numbers a two-dimensional array is used. This chapter presents some interesting challenges realted with 2D arrays.

## Challenge 69

Write a program to obtain transpose of 3 x 3 matrix.

## Solution

*(handwritten margin note: In order to transpose a matrix Index it Create a matrix [3][3])*

```c
/* Transpose of a matrix */
#include <stdio.h>
#define ROWS 3
#define COLS 3

void create ( int [ ROWS ][ COLS ] ) ;
void display ( int [ ROWS ][ COLS ] ) ;
void transpose ( int [ ROWS ][ COLS ], int [ ROWS ][ COLS ] ) ;

int main( )
{
    int  mat1[ ROWS ][ COLS ], mat2[ ROWS ][ COLS ] ;

    printf ( "Enter array elements:\n\n" ) ;
    create ( mat1 ) ;

    transpose ( mat1, mat2 ) ;
    printf ( "Transpose of matrix:\n" ) ;
    display ( mat2 ) ;

    return 0 ;
}

/* creates matrix mat */
void create ( int  mat[ ROWS ][ COLS ] )
{
    int  i, j ;

    for ( i = 0 ; i < ROWS ; i++ )
    {
        for ( j = 0 ; j < COLS ; j++ )
        {
            printf ( "Enter the element: " ) ;
```

```
            scanf ( "%d", &mat[ i ][ j ] ) ;
        }
    }
    printf ( "\n" ) ;
}

/* displays the contents of matrix */
void display ( int  mat[ ROWS ][ COLS ] )
{
    int  i, j ;

    for ( i = 0 ; i < ROWS ; i++ )
    {
        for ( j = 0 ; j < COLS ; j++ )
            printf ( "%d\t", mat[ i ][ j ] ) ;
        printf ( "\n" ) ;
    }
}

/* obtains transpose of matrix m1 */
void transpose ( int  m1[ ROWS ][ COLS ], int  m2[ ROWS ][ COLS ] )
{
    int  i, j ;

    for ( i = 0 ; i < ROWS ; i++ )
    {
        for ( j = 0 ; j < COLS ; j++ )
            m2[ i ][ j ] = m1[ j ][ i ] ;
    }
}
```

## Sample Run

Enter array elements:

Enter the element: 1
Enter the element: 2
Enter the element: 3
Enter the element: 4
Enter the element: 5
Enter the element: 6

Enter the element: 7
Enter the element: 8
Enter the element: 9

Transpose of matrix:
1    4    7
2    5    8
3    6    9

## Explanation

In this program the function **create( )** is used to create an 2D array (matrix) of **int**s. The **display( )** function displays the elements of the matrix.

The function **transpose( )**, transposes a matrix. A transpose of a matrix is obtained by interchanging the rows with corresponding columns of a given matrix. Note how **m1** and **m2** have been declared inf the **transpose( )** function. This is the way to receive a 2D array passed to a function. The transposed matrix is stored in **mat2**.

## Challenge 70

Write a program to obtain sum of two 3 x 3 matrices.

## Solution

```
/* Addition of matrices */
#include <stdio.h>
#define ROWS 3
#define COLS 3

void create ( int [ ROWS ][ COLS ] ) ;
void display ( int [ ROWS ][ COLS ] ) ;
void matadd ( int [ ROWS ][ COLS ], int [ ROWS ][ COLS ],
              int [ ROWS ][ COLS ] ) ;

int main( )
{
```

```
    int  mat1[ ROWS ][ COLS ], mat2[ ROWS ][ COLS ] ;
    int  mat3[ ROWS ][ COLS ] ; ;

    printf ( "Enter elements for first array:\n\n" ) ;
    create ( mat1 ) ;

    printf ( "Enter elements for second array:\n\n" ) ;
    create ( mat2 ) ;

    printf ( "First Array:\n" ) ;
    display ( mat1 ) ;
    printf ( "Second Array:\n" ) ;
    display ( mat2 ) ;

    matadd ( mat1, mat2, mat3 ) ;
    printf ( "After Addition:\n" ) ;
    display ( mat3 ) ;

    return 0 ;
}

/* creates matrix mat */
void create ( int mat[ ROWS ][ COLS ] )
{
    int  i, j ;

    for ( i = 0 ; i < ROWS ; i++ )
    {
        for ( j = 0 ; j < COLS ; j++ )
        {
            printf ( "Enter the element: " ) ;
            scanf ( "%d", &mat[ i ][ j ] ) ;
        }
    }
    printf ( "\n" ) ;
}

/* displays the contents of matrix */
void display ( int mat[ ROWS ][ COLS ] )
{
    int  i, j ;
```

```
        for ( i = 0 ; i < ROWS ; i++ )
        {
            for ( j = 0 ; j < COLS ; j++ )
                printf ( "%d\t", mat[ i ][ j ] ) ;
            printf ( "\n" ) ;
        }
    }

    /* adds two matrices m1 and m2 */
    void matadd ( int  m1[ ROWS ][ COLS ], int  m2[ ROWS ][ COLS ],
                    int  m3[ ROWS ][ COLS ] )
    {
        int  i, j ;

        for ( i = 0 ; i < ROWS ; i++ )
        {
            for ( j = 0 ; j < COLS ; j++ )
                m3[ i ][ j ] = m1[ i ][ j ] + m2[ i ][ j ] ;
        }
    }
```

## Sample Run

Enter elements for first array:

Enter the element: 1
Enter the element: 1
Enter the element: 1
Enter the element: 1
Enter the element: 1
Enter the element: 1
Enter the element: 1
Enter the element: 1
Enter the element: 1

Enter elements for second array:

Enter the element: 2
Enter the element: 2
Enter the element: 2

Enter the element: 2
Enter the element: 2
Enter the element: 2
Enter the element: 2
Enter the element: 2
Enter the element: 2

First Array:
1    1    1
1    1    1
1    1    1
Second Array:
2    2    2
2    2    2
2    2    2
After Addition:
3    3    3
3    3    3
3    3    3

## Explanation

In this program the function **create( )** is used to create an 2D array (matrix) of **int**s. The **display( )** function displays the elements of the matrix.

The function **matadd( )** adds the elements of two matrices **mat1** and **mat2** and stores the result in the third matrix **mat3**. Note that usually two **for** loops would be used to access all the elements of a 2D array.

## Challenge 71

Write a program to obtain product of two 3 x 3 matrices.

Index it

## Solution

```c
/* Multiplication of matrices */
#include <stdio.h>
#define ROWS 3
```

```
#define COLS 3

void create ( int [ ROWS ][ COLS ] ) ;
void display ( int [ ROWS ][ COLS ] ) ;
void matmul ( int [ ROWS ][ COLS ], int [ ROWS ][ COLS ],
              int [ ROWS ][ COLS ] ) ;

int main( )
{
    int  mat1[ ROWS ][ COLS ], mat2[ ROWS ][ COLS ] ;
    int  mat3[ ROWS ][ COLS ] ;

    printf ( "Enter elements for first array:\n\n" ) ;
    create ( mat1 ) ;

    printf ( "Enter elements for second array:\n\n" ) ;
    create ( mat2 ) ;

    printf ( "First Array:\n" ) ;
    display ( mat1 ) ;
    printf ( "Second Array:\n" ) ;
    display ( mat2 ) ;

    matmul ( mat1, mat2, mat3 ) ;
    printf ( "After Addition:\n" ) ;
    display ( mat3 ) ;

    return 0 ;
}

/* creates matrix mat */
void create ( int  mat[ ROWS ][ COLS ] )
{
    int  i, j ;

    for ( i = 0 ; i < ROWS ; i++ )
    {
        for ( j = 0 ; j < COLS ; j++ )
        {
            printf ( "Enter the element: " ) ;
            scanf ( "%d", &mat[ i ][ j ] ) ;
```

```
        }
    }
    printf ( "\n" ) ;
}

/* displays the contents of matrix */
void display ( int  mat[ ROWS ][ COLS ] )
{
    int  i, j ;

    for ( i = 0 ; i < ROWS ; i++ )
    {
        for ( j = 0 ; j < COLS ; j++ )
            printf ( "%d\t", mat[ i ][ j ] ) ;
        printf ( "\n" ) ;
    }
}

/* multiplies two matrices m1 and m2 */
void matmul ( int  m1[ ROWS ][ COLS ], int  m2[ ROWS ][ COLS ],
              int  m3[ ROWS ][ COLS ] )
{
    int  i, j, k ;

    for ( k = 0 ; k < ROWS ; k++ )
    {
        for ( i = 0 ; i < COLS ; i++ )
        {
            m3[ k ][ i ] = 0 ;
            for ( j = 0 ; j < COLS ; j++ )
                m3[ k ][ i ] += m1[ k ][ j ] * m2[ j ][ i ] ;
        }
    }
}
```

*[handwritten annotations:]* 3 — Each element of Row each element of column 3×3 3×3×3 ↦ [K][ ] [ ][ ] [K][J] [J][i] R  C  C  C

Enter elements for first array:

Enter the element: 1
Enter the element: 1

Enter the element: 1
Enter the element: 1
Enter the element: 1
Enter the element: 1
Enter the element: 1
Enter the element: 1
Enter the element: 1

Enter elements for second array:

Enter the element: 2
Enter the element: 2
Enter the element: 2
Enter the element: 2
Enter the element: 2
Enter the element: 2
Enter the element: 2
Enter the element: 2
Enter the element: 2

First Array:
1    1    1
1    1    1
1    1    1
Second Array:
2    2    2
2    2    2
2    2    2
After Addition:
6    6    6
6    6    6
6    6    6

## Explanation

In this program the function **create( )** is used to create an 2D array (matrix) of **int**s. The **display( )** function displays the elements of the matrix.

The function **matmul( )** multiplies the elements of matrix **mat1** with the elements of matrix **mat2** and stores the result in **mat4.**

In **matmul( )** the third **for** loop multiplies each element of a given row with corresponding elements of a given column. The given row and col are generated by the first and the second **for** loop respectively.

## Challenge 72

Given a 2D array, write a program to visit all its elements in a spiral fashion. For example, for the array given below

{ 1, 2, 3, 4 }
{ 5, 6, 7, 8 }
{ 9, 10, 11, 12 }
{ 13, 14, 15,16 }

The elements should be visited in the order:

1 2 3 4 8 12 16 15 14 13 9 5 6 7 11 10

## Solution

```
#include <stdio.h>
#define ROWS 4
#define COLS 4

int main( )
{
    int arr[ ROWS ][ COLS ] = {
                            { 1, 2, 3, 4 },
                            { 5, 6, 7, 8 },
                            { 9, 10, 11, 12 },
                            { 13, 14, 15,16 }
                    } ;
    int i ;
    int toprow, bottomrow, leftcol, rightcol ;

    toprow = 0 ;
    bottomrow = ROWS - 1 ;
    leftcol = 0 ;
    rightcol = COLS - 1 ;

    while ( toprow <= bottomrow && leftcol <= rightcol )
    {
```

*leP to right*

```
for ( i = leftcol ; i <= rightcol ; i++ )
    printf ( "%d ", arr[ toprow ][ i ] ) ;
toprow++ ;
```

*1st row*
*Last col*

*Top to bottom*

```
for ( i = toprow ; i <= bottomrow ; i++ )
    printf ( "%d ", arr[ i ][ rightcol ] ) ;
rightcol-- ;
```

*2nd row*
*last col*

*right to left*

```
for ( i = rightcol ; i >= leftcol ; i-- )
    printf ( "%d ", arr[ bottomrow ][ i ] ) ;

bottomrow-- ;
```

*3rd row*
*2nd last col*

*2nd row*

*bottom to top*

```
    for ( i = bottomrow ; i >= toprow ; i-- )
        printf ( "%d ", arr[ i ][ leftcol ] ) ;
    leftcol++ ;
}
```

```
    return 0 ;
}
```

## Sample Run

1 2 3 4 8 12 16 15 14 13 9 5 6 7 11 10

## Explanation

The program moves through the matrix using 4 **for** loops. The first one moves from left to right, second from top to bottom, third from right to left and fourth from bottom to top. These loops are executed till **toprow** doesn't cross the **bottomrow** and **leftcol** doesn't cross the **rightcol**.

You can change the values of ROWS, COLS and correspondingly the values in the array and execute it for different-sized matrices.

## Challenge 73

Given a matrix that contains only 1s and/or 0s, write a program to obtain the order of largest square sub-matrix with all 1s.

## Solution

```c
/* Obtain order of largest square sub-matrix with all 1s */
#include <stdio.h>
#define ROW 5
#define COL 5

int max1submatrix ( int [ ROW ][ COL ] ) ;

int main ( )
{
    int  arr[ ROW ][ COL ] = {
                                { 1, 0, 0, 1, 1 },
                                { 0, 1, 1, 1, 0 },
                                { 1, 1, 1, 1, 1 },
                                { 0, 1, 1, 1, 0 },
                                { 0, 0, 0, 1, 1 }
                            } ;
    int  max1 ;

    max1 = max1submatrix ( arr ) ;
    printf ( "Order of largest sqr. sub-mat. with all 1s = %d\n", max1 ) ;
}

int max1submatrix ( int  arr[ ROW ][ COL ] )
{
    int  aux[ ROW ][ COL ] = { 0 } ;
    int  i, j, min, max ;

    int minimum ( int, int, int ) ;

    for ( i = 0 ; i < COL ; i++ )
        aux[ 0 ][ i ] = arr[ 0 ][ i ] ;

    for ( i = 0 ; i < ROW ; i++ )
        aux[ i ][ 0 ] = arr[ i ][ 0 ] ;

    for ( i = 1 ; i < ROW ; i++ )
    {
        for ( j = 1 ; j < COL ; j++ )
```

```
        {
            if ( arr[ i ][ j ] == 1 )
            {
                min = minimum ( aux[ i - 1 ][ j - 1 ], aux[ i ][ j - 1 ],
                                aux[ i - 1 ][ j ] ) ;
                aux[ i ][ j ] = min + 1 ;
            }
            else
                aux[ i ][ j ] = 0 ;
        }
    }

    max = 0 ;
    for ( i = 0 ; i < ROW ; i++ )
    {
        for ( j = 0 ; j < COL ; j++ )
        {
            if ( aux[ i ][ j ] > max )
                max = aux[ i ][ j ] ;
        }
    }

    return max ;
}

int minimum ( int  a, int  b, int  c )
{
    int  min ;

    min = a ;

    if ( b < min )
        min = b ;

    if ( c < min )
        min = c ;

    return min ;
}
```

## Sample Run

Order of largest square submatrix with all 1s = 3

## Explanation

To find the order of the largest square submatrix with all 1s we have used one more matrix **aux[ ][ ]**. If **arr[ i ][ j ]** is the rightmost and the bottommost entry of the largest square submatrix with all 1s, then finally **aux[ i ][ j ]** would contain the size of the largest square submatrix with all 1s. To achieve this, we have followed the following procedure:

We set zeroth row and zeroth column of **aux[ ][ ]** to be the same as **arr[ ][ ]**. Then starting from the first row, and first column, if **arr[ i ][ j ]** is 0, then the bottommost and rightmost entry in the possible sub-matrix would be 0, which is not possible (because minimum size of the desired sub-matrix would be 1) so, we store 0 in **aux[ i ][ j ]**.

If **arr[ i ] [ j ]** is 1, then obtain the minimum value present in **aux[ ][ ]** out of elements present above, to the left, and in the upper diagonal of **aux[ i ][ j ]**. Add 1 to this minimum value and store it in **aux[ i ][ j ]**.

That is, if the values at top, left and upper diagonal in **aux[ ][ ]** are all 0, it means that the values in **arr[ ][ ]** at top, left and upper diagonal are 0. In this case even though **arr[ i ][ j ]** is 1, the maximum size of square sub-matrix whose rightmost and bottommost element is **arr[ i ][ j ]**, would be 1.

In our example, for **aux[ 2 ][ 2 ]**, the left, top and upper diagonal values of **aux[ ][ ]** are all 1, which means that the value of **arr[ ][ ]** at these 3 places is 1, so that combined with **arr[ 2 ][ 2 ]** will give rise to square sub-matrix of all 1s of size 2 and ending at **arr[ 2 ][ 2 ]**.

# 10 / Total Challenges: 13

# String Challenges

The way a group of integers can be stored in an integer array, likewise a group of characters can be stored in a character array. Character arrays are often called 'strings'. They are used by programming languages to manipulate text such as words and sentences. This chapter present several challenges related with their access and storage.

153

## Challenge 74

Write a program to implement the following functions:

strlen: Finds the length of the string

strcpy: Copies contents of one string to another string

strcat: Appends one string at the end of another string

strcmp:Compares two strings to find whether they are identical or not

## Solution

```c
/* Implements different string functions */
#include <stdio.h>

int xstrlen ( char * ) ;
void xstrcpy ( char *, char * ) ;
void xstrcat ( char *, char * ) ;
int xstrcmp ( char *, char * ) ;
void show ( char * ) ;

int main( )
{
    char  s1[ ] = "kicit" ;
    char  s2[ ] = "Nagpur" ;
    char  s3[ 20 ] ;
    int  len ;

    printf ( "String s1: %s\n", s1 ) ;
    len = xstrlen ( s1 ) ;
    printf ( "length of the string s1: %d\n", len ) ;

    printf ( "String s2: %s\n", s2 ) ;

    xstrcpy ( s3, s1 ) ;
    printf ( "String s3 after copying s1 to it: %s\n", s3 ) ;

    xstrcat ( s3, s2 ) ;
    printf ( "String s3 after concatenation: %s\n", s3 ) ;
```

```
    if ( xstrcmp ( s1, s2 ) == 0 )
        printf ( "The strings s1 and s2 are similar\n" ) ;
    else
        printf ( "The strings s1 and s2 are not similar\n" ) ;

    return 0 ;
}

/* finds the length of the string */
int xstrlen ( char  *s )
{
    int I = 0 ;

    while ( *s )
    {
        I++ ;
        s++ ;
    }
    return ( I ) ;
}
```

*Custom version of len*

```
/* copies source string s to the target string t */
void xstrcpy ( char *t, char  *s )
{
    while ( *s )
    {
        *t = *s ;
        t++ ;
        s++ ;
    }
    *t = '\0' ;
}
```

*Custom version of strcpy*

```
/* concatenates the two strings */
void xstrcat ( char *t, char  *s )
{
    while ( *t )
        t++ ;

    while ( *s )
```

*Custom version of strcat*

```
    {
        *t = *s ;
        t++ ;
        s++ ;
    }

    *t = '\0' ;
}

/* compares two strings s and t for equality */
int xstrcmp ( char *s, char *t )
{
    while ( *s == *t )
    {
        if ( *s == '\0' )
            break ;
        s++ ;
        t++ ;
    }
    return ( *s - *t ) ;
}
```

 custom version of strcmp

## Sample Run

String s1: kicit
length of the string s1: 5
String s2: Nagpur
String s3 after copying s1 to it: kicit
String s3 after concatenation: kicitNagpur
The strings s1 and s2 are not similar

## Explanation

In this program we have created three arrays of characters, **s1**, **s2** and **s3**.

The function **xstrlen( )** is fairly simple. It receives only one parameter—the base address of a string. All that it does is, it keeps counting the characters till the end of string is not met. Or in other words, it keeps counting characters till the pointer **s** doesn't point to '\0'.

The function **xstrcpy( )** receives two parameters. These parameters are the base addresses of the target and source strings respectively. This function copies the source string whose base address is received in pointer **s**, to the target string whose base address is received in the pointer **t**. The function goes on copying the source string into the target string till it doesn't encounter the end of source string. Once the end of source string is reached, a '\0' is stored at the end of the target string. It is our responsibility to see to it that target string's dimension is big enough to hold the string being copied into it.

The function **xstrcat( )** also receives two parameters. Here also the parameters are the pointers to the base addresses of the target and source strings respectively. This function adds the source string whose base address is stored in pointer **s** at the end of target string whose base address is stored in pointer **t**. In the first **while** loop we have made the pointer **t** to point to the end of the string. In the second **while** loop the contents of source string pointed to by **s** are added character by character to the target string pointed to by **t**. Lastly, we have added a null terminating character '\0' at the end of the target string pointed to by **t**.

Another useful string function is **xstrcmp( )** which compares two strings to find out whether they are same or different. The two strings **s1** and **s2** pointed to by **s** and **t** respectively, are compared character by character until there is a mismatch or end of one of the string is reached, whichever occurs first. If the two strings are identical, **xstrcmp( )** function returns a 0. Otherwise, it returns the numeric difference between the **ASCII** values of the first non-matching pair of characters.

## Challenge 75 *Index it*

Write a program that extracts a string from the left, right or middle of a string.

## Solution

```
#include <stdio.h>
#include <string.h>
#include <stdlib.h>

#define WRONG 0
```

*In case of a M/s -match, return the numeric difference between ASCII values of p the first non-matching Pair of Character.*

```
#define CORRECT 1

char * getsub ( char *, int, int ) ;
char * leftsub ( char *, int ) ;
char * rightsub ( char *, int ) ;

int main ( )
{
    char  str[ ] = "Four hundred and thirty two" ;
    char  *s ;

    printf ( "String: %s\n", str ) ;

    s = getsub ( str, 5, 7 ) ;
    if ( s != NULL )
    {
        printf ( "Substring: %s\n", s ) ;
        free ( s ) ;
    }

    s = leftsub ( str, 4 ) ;
    if ( s != NULL )
    {
        printf ( "Left substring: %s\n", s ) ;
        free ( s ) ;
    }

    s = rightsub ( str, 3 ) ;
    if ( s != NULL )
    {
        printf ( "Right substring: %s\n", s ) ;
        free ( s ) ;
    }

    return 0 ;
}

char* getsub ( char *str, int  spos, int  n )
{
    int  len, input, i ;
    char  *t ;
```

*[handwritten note: Freeing Memory after printing each Substring]*

```
    input = CORRECT ;
    len = strlen ( str ) ;

    if ( spos < 0 || spos >= len )
    {
        input = WRONG ;
        printf ( "Starting index out of range\n" ) ;
    }
    else if ( len <= 0 )
    {
        input = WRONG ;
        printf ( "Length of substring specified invalid\n" ) ;
    }
    else if ( spos + n - 1 >= len )
    {
        input = WRONG ;
        printf ( "Length out of range\n" ) ;
    }
    else
    {
        t = ( char* ) malloc ( n + 1 ) ;

        for ( i = 0 ; i < n ; i++ )
            t[ i ] = str[ spos + i ] ;

        t[ i ] = '\0' ;
    }

    if ( input == WRONG )
        return NULL ;
    else
        return ( t ) ;
}

char* leftsub ( char *str, int  n )
{
    int  len, input, i ;
    char  *t ;

    input = CORRECT ;
```

— Allocating memory based on no of characters to be extracted

```
        len = strlen ( str ) ;

        if ( n < 0 || n > len )
        {
            input = WRONG ;
            printf ( "Length of left substring specified invalid\n" ) ;
        }
        else
        {
            t = ( char* ) malloc ( n + 1 ) ;

            for ( i = 0 ; i < n ; i++ )
                t[ i ] = str[ i ] ;

            t[ i ] = '\0' ;
        }

        if ( input == WRONG )
            return NULL ;
        else
            return ( t ) ;
}

char* rightsub ( char *str, int n )
{
    int  len, input, i ;
    char  *t ;

    len = strlen ( str ) ;
    input = CORRECT ;

    if ( n < 0 || n > len )
    {
        input = WRONG ;
        printf ( "Length of right substring specified invalid. \n" ) ;
    }
    else
    {
        t = ( char* ) malloc ( n + 1 ) ;
```

*(handwritten note:)* — Allocating Memory based on no of character to be extracted

*(handwritten note:)* — Allocating memory based on no of character to be extracted

```
        for ( i = 0 ; i < n ; i++ )
            t[ n - i - 1 ] = str[ len - i - 1 ];

        t[ n ] = '\0' ;
    }

    if ( input == WRONG )
        return NULL ;
    else
        return ( t ) ;
}
```

$$t[3-0-1] = str[23-0-1]$$
$$t[3-1-1] = str[23-1-1]$$
$$t[3-2-1] = str[23-2-1]$$

$$t[2] = 'o'$$
$$t[1] = 'w'$$
$$t[0] = 't'$$

## Sample Run

String str: Four hundred thirty two
Sub string: hundred
Left sub string: Four
Right sub string: two

## Explanation

The functions (getsub( ), leftsub( ) and rightsub( ) are used to extract specified number of characters from a specified position in a string. They differ only in the starting position from which the characters are to be extracted.

The function getsub( ) receives three parameters. The first is the base address of the string from which the characters are to be extracted. The second is the starting position of the string from where the extraction should begin and the third is the number of characters to be extracted.

Both the functions **leftsub( )** and **rightsub( )** receive two parameters that represents the base address of the string and the number of characters to be extracted from the left side or right side of the string respectively. Note that none of these three functions make any changes to the contents of the string from which characters are being extracted. Instead, they create a new string **t** by allocating new memory of sufficient size and returns **t** as a final result of the extraction operation.

## Challenge 76

Write a program that counts vowels, consonants and words present in a sentence that is received from the keyboard.

### Solution

```c
/* Count vowels, consonants and words in a sentence */
#include <stdio.h>

int main( )
{
    char  str[ 80 ] ;
    int  vows, consos, words ;
    char *s, *t ;

    printf ( "Enter a sentence not more than 80 characters long:\n" ) ;
    fgets ( str, 80, stdin ) ;

    vows = consos = words = 0 ;

    s = str ;
    while ( *s != '\0' )
    {
        if ( isalpha ( *s ) )
        {
            switch ( *s )
            {
                case 'a' :
                case 'e' :
                case 'i' :
                case 'o' :
                case 'u' :
                case 'A' :
                case 'E' :
                case 'I' :
                case 'O' :
                case 'U' :
                    vows++ ;
```

```
                break ;

            default :
                consos++ ;
            }
        s++ ;
    }
    else if ( isspace ( *s ) )
    {
        words++ ;
        while ( isspace ( *s ) )
            s++ ;
    }
    else
        s++ ;
    }

    printf ( "Vowels = %d\n", vows ) ;
    printf ( "Consonants = %d\n", consos ) ;
    printf ( "Words = %d\n", words ) ;

    return 0 ;
}
```

→ checke for the Possibility when there are multiple spaces between words

## Sample Run

Enter a sentence not more than 80 characters long:
Able was I ere I saw elba
Vowels = 10
Consonants = 9
Words = 7

## Explanation

**isalpha( )** is a library function that checks whether a character is an alphabet or not. If it found so, then through a **switch** we have checked if the alphabet is a vowel or a consonant.

If **isalpha( )** finds that the character is not an alphabet, then the **isspace( )** function is used to check whether the character is a space or not. If it is a space then the **while** loop goes to the next non-blank character. Once it reaches the non-blank character we increment the word count. This accounts for the possibility that there are multiple spaces between words and word count is not incremented every time we come across a space.

## Challenge 77

Write a program to delete all vowels from a sentence. Assume that the sentence is not more than 80 characters long.

## Solution

```c
/* Delete all vowels from a sentence */
#include <stdio.h>

int main( )
{
    char  str[ 80 ], str1[ 80 ] ;
    char  *s, *t ;

    printf ( "Enter a sentence not more than 80 characters long:\n" ) ;
    fgets ( str, 80, stdin ) ;

    s = str ;
    t = str1 ;

    while ( *s != '\0' )
    {
        switch ( *s )
        {
            case 'a' :
            case 'e' :
            case 'i' :
            case 'o' :
            case 'u' :
            case 'A' :
            case 'E' :
            case 'I' :
            case 'O' :
            case 'U' :
```

*Index it*

*usage of fgets to read character into a char array*

```
            s++ ;
            break ;

        default :
            *t = *s ;
            s++ ;
            t++ ;
    }
}
*t = '\0' ;

printf ( "Sentence after removing all vowels:\n%s\n", str1 ) ;

return 0 ;
}
```

## Sample Run

Enter a sentence not more than 80 characters long:
A sentence cannot start with because.
Sentence after removing all vowels is:
 sntnc cnnt strt wth bcs.

## Explanation

The program traverses the source string **str** using a **while** loop, looking for vowels. If it comes across a vowel, it simply goes to the next character in the string. As against this, if it comes across a character other than a vowel, it copies it into the target string **str1**.

Note two things in the program:

(a) Usage of pointers to copy characters from source string **str** to target string **str1**. Had we not used pointers we would have been required to use an index variable for the arrays and increment it every time we copy a character.

(b) Usage of **fgets( )** to read a string from keyboard (**stdin**). This is a safer method than **gets( )** because it stops reading the string beyond 80 characters. This prevents accidently exceeding the bounds of a string.

## Challenge 78

Write a program to reverse the strings stored in the following 2D array of characters:

```
char s[ ][ 100 ] = {
                    "To err is human...",
                    "But to really mess things up...",
                    "One needs to know C!!"
                } ;
```

## Solution

```c
/* Reverse strings stored in a 2D array */
#include <stdio.h>
#include <string.h>

void strreverse ( char * ) ;

int main( )
{
    char s[ ][ 100 ] = {
                        "To err is human",
                        "But to really mess things up",
                        "One needs to know C"
                    } ;
    int  i ;

    for ( i = 0 ; i < 3 ; i++ )
    {
        strreverse ( s[ i ] ) ;
        printf ( "%s\n", s[ i ] ) ;
    }

    return 0 ;
}

void strreverse ( char  *str )
{
    int  begin, end ;
```

*Index it* ✓

→ *Processes one row of text at a time*

```
begin = 0 ;
end = strlen ( str ) - 1 ;

while ( begin < end )
{
    char ch = str[ begin ] ;         — temp storage
    str[ begin ] = str[ end ] ;
    str[ end ] = ch ;

    begin++ ;
    end-- ;
}
}
```

## Sample Run

```
namuh si rre oT
pu sgniht ssem yllaer ot tuB
C wonk ot sdeen enO
```

## Explanation

The **strreverse( )** function sets up two indexes—**begin** and **end** at the beginning and end of the string respectively. Then it goes on exchanging character present in the string at positions **begin** and **end**. The process stops when **begin** equals **end**.

The **strreverse( )** function is called once for each string present in array **s[ ][ ]**.

## Challenge 79

Write a program that generates and prints the Fibonacci words of order 0 through 5. If f(0) = "a", f(1) = "b", f(2) = "ba", f(3) = "bab", f(4) = "babba", etc.

*Indent*

## Solution

```
/* Generate Fibonacci words of order 0 through 5 */
```

str fib[20]

strcpy [s2, 'b']
strcat [s2,

```c
#include <stdio.h>
#include <string.h>

int main( )
{
    char  str[ 50 ] ;
    char  lastbutoneterm[ 50 ] = "A" ;
    char  lastterm[ 50 ] = "B" ;
    int  i ;

    for ( i = 1 ; i <= 5 ; i++ )
    {
        strcpy ( str, lastterm ) ;
        strcat ( str, lastbutoneterm ) ;
        printf ( "%s\n", str ) ;

        strcpy ( lastbutoneterm, lastterm ) ;
        strcpy ( lastterm, str ) ;
    }

    return 0 ;
}
```

## Sample Run

```
a
b
ba
bab
babba
```

## Explanation

**strcpy( )** function copies source string to target string, whereas **strcat( )** concatenates (appends) source string at the end of target string. These functions are effectively used to build the sequence of Fibonacci words.

## Challenge 80

A Credit Card number is usually a 16-digit number. A valid Credit Card number would satisfy a rule explained below with the help of a dummy Credit Card number—4567 1234 5678 9129. Start with the rightmost - 1 digit and multiply every other digit by 2.

4567  1234  5 678  9 1 2 9  — 16

8 12   2  6   10 14   18   4

Then subtract 9 from any number larger than 10. Thus we get:

8 3 2 6 1 5 9 4

Add them all up to get 38.

Add all the other digits to get 42.

Sum of 38 and 42 is 80. Since 80 is divisible by 10, the Credit Card number is valid.

Write a program that receives a Credit Card number and checks using the above rule whether the Credit Card number is valid.

## Solution

```
/* Verify correctness of Credit Card Number */
#include <stdio.h>
#define WRONG 0
#define CORRECT 1

int main ( )
{
    char  str[ 16 ] ;
    int  input, i, digit, sum, multiple ;

    input = CORRECT ;
    sum = 0 ;

    printf ( "Enter a 16 digit credit card number:\n" ) ;
    scanf ( "%s", str ) ;
```

```c
for ( i = 15 ; i >= 0 ; i-- )
{
    if ( str[ i ] < '0' || str[ i ] > '9' )
    {
        input = WRONG ;
        break ;
    }
    else
    {
        digit = str[ i ] - '0' ;
        if ( i % 2 == 0 )
        {
            multiple = digit * 2 ;
            if ( multiple >= 10 )
                digit = multiple - 9 ;
            else
                digit = multiple ;
        }

        sum = sum + digit ;
    }
}

if ( input == WRONG )
    printf ( "Credit card number must contain only digits\n" ) ;
else
{
    if ( sum % 10 == 0 )
        printf ( "Credit card number is valid\n" ) ;
    else
        printf ( "Credit card number is invalid\n" ) ;
}
return 0 ;
}
```

## Sample Runs

Enter a 16 digit credit card number:
4181 3620 0022 8855
Credit card number is valid

```
Enter a 16 digit credit card number:
1234567898765432
Credit card number is invalid
```

## Explanation

Since the Credit Card number is received as a string, each digit present in it is stored as ASCII value of the digit. Hence while doing arithmetic, each character is first converted into a number by subtracting ASCII value of 0 from it.

Note the way the program checks for wrong input using the macros. Rest of the program is pretty straight-forward.

## Challenge 81

To uniquely identify a book a 10-digit ISBN number is used. The ISBN number is considered to be correct if the sum $d_1 + 2d_2 + 3d_3 + ... + 10d_{10}$ is a multiple of 11 (where $d_i$ denotes the $i^{th}$ digit from the right). The digits $d_2$ to $d_9$ can take any value from 0 to 9, whereas $d_1$ can be any value from 0 to 10. The ISBN convention is to use the value X to denote 10. Write a program that receives a 10-character ISBN number and reports whether the ISBN number is correct or not.

Index it

## Solution

```c
#include <stdio.h>
#define CORRECT 1
#define WRONG 0

int main( )                  ← should be 10 + 2
{
    char str[ 10 ];
    int sum, i, digit, input, weight ;

    printf ( "Enter an ISBN number: \n" ) ;
    scanf ( "%s", str ) ;

    sum = 0 ;
    input = CORRECT ;
```

```
weight = 10 ;

for ( i = 0 ; i <= 8 ; i++ )
{
    if ( str[ i ] >= '0' || str[ i ] <= '9' )
    {
        digit = str[ i ] - '0' ;
        sum = sum + weight * digit ;
        weight-- ;
    }
    else
    {
        input = WRONG ;
        break ;
    }
}

if ( input == CORRECT )
{
    if ( str[ 9 ] >= '0' && str[ 9 ] <= '9' )
    {
        digit = str[ i ] - '0' ;
        sum = sum + digit ;
    }
    else if ( str[ 9 ] == 'x' || str[ 9 ] == 'X' )
    {
        digit = 10 ;
        sum = sum + digit ;
    }
    else
        input = WRONG ;
}

if ( input == WRONG )
    printf ( "Invalid input\n" ) ;
else
{
    if ( sum % 11 == 0 )
        printf ( "ISBN number verified and found to be correct\n" ) ;
    else
        printf ( "Checksum error in ISBN number\n" ) ;
```

*(handwritten note, right): checks first 9 Number in ISBN*

*(handwritten note, left): break statements are always used inside loops to break out of*

*(handwritten note, right): To check for the possibility that 10th digit in ISBN might be the character 'x' or '0'*

```
    }
    return 0 ;
}
```

## Sample Runs

```
Enter an ISBN number:
1572224940
ISBN number verified and found to be correct

Enter an ISBN number:
1572225181
ISBN number verified and found to be correct
```

## Explanation

The program first gets weighted sum of digits $d_1$ to $d_9$ in a **for** loop. Then it adds $d_{10}$ to the weighted sum and checks if it is divisible by 11.

Note that the program considers the possibility of wrong input as well as $d_{10}$ being a digit or character x.

## Challenge 82

Write a program that receives the month and year from the keyboard as integers and prints the calendar in the following format.

| | | December 2016 | | | | |
| --- | --- | --- | --- | --- | --- | --- |
| Mon | Tue | Wed | Thu | Fri | Sat | Sun |
| | | | 1 | 2 | 3 | 4 |
| 5 | 6 | 7 | 8 | 9 | 10 | 11 |
| 12 | 13 | 14 | 15 | 16 | 17 | 18 |
| 19 | 20 | 21 | 22 | 23 | 24 | 25 |
| 26 | 27 | 28 | 29 | 30 | 31 | |

Note that according to the Gregorian calendar 01/01/01 was Monday. With this as the base, the calendar should be generated.

## Solution

```
/* Program to display calendar of any year */
# include <stdio.h>
void gotoxy ( int  col, int  row ) ;

int main( )
{
    char  *months[ ] = {
                         "January", "February", "March",
                         "April", "May", "June",
                         "July", "August", "September",
                         "October", "November", "December"
                       } ;
    int  days[ 12 ] = { 31, 28, 31, 30, 31, 30, 31, 31, 30, 31, 30, 31 } ;
    long int  ndays, ldays, tdays ;
    int  m, y, sum, fday, i, r, c ;

    printf ( "Enter year & month:\n" ) ;
    scanf ( "%d %d", &y, &m ) ;

    ndays = ( y - 1 ) * 365l ;
    ldays = ( y - 1 ) / 4 - ( y - 1 ) / 100 + ( y - 1 ) / 400 ;
    tdays = ndays + ldays ;

    if ( ( ( y % 400 == 0 ) || ( y % 100 != 0 && y % 4 == 0 ) )
        days[ 1 ] = 29 ;
    else
        days[ 1 ] = 28 ;

    sum = 0 ;
    for ( i = 0 ; i <= m - 2 ; i++ )
        sum = sum + days[ i ] ;

    tdays = tdays + sum ;
    fday = tdays % 7 ;

    system ( "clear" ) ;
    gotoxy ( 25, 2 ) ;
    printf ( "%s %d", months[ m - 1 ], y ) ;
```

```
    gotoxy ( 5, 5 ) ;
    printf ( "-------------------------------------------------" ) ;

    gotoxy ( 10, 6 ) ;
    printf ( "Mon  Tue  Wed  Thu  Fri  Sat  Sun" ) ;

    gotoxy ( 5, 7 ) ;
    printf ( "-------------------------------------------------" ) ;

    r = 9 ;
    c = 11 + 6 * fday ;
    for ( i = 1 ; i <= days[ m - 1 ] ; i++ )
    {
        gotoxy ( c, r ) ;
        printf ( "%d", i ) ;

        if ( c <= 41 )
            c = c + 6 ;
        else
        {
            c = 11 ;
            r = r + 1 ;
        }
    }

    gotoxy ( 5, 15 ) ;
    printf ( "-------------------------------------------------\n" ) ;

    return 0 ;
}

void gotoxy ( int  x, int  y )
{
    printf ( "%c[%d;%df", 0x1B, y, x ) ;
}
```

## Sample Run

|  | | | July 2015 | | | |
| --- | --- | --- | --- | --- | --- | --- |
| Mon | Tue | Wed | Thu | Fri | Sat | Sun |
|  |  | 1 | 2 | 3 | 4 | 5 |
| 6 | 7 | 8 | 9 | 10 | 11 | 12 |
| 13 | 14 | 15 | 16 | 17 | 18 | 19 |
| 20 | 21 | 22 | 23 | 24 | 25 | 26 |
| 27 | 28 | 29 | 30 | 31 |  |  |

## Explanation

To understand the program let us assume that we wish to generate the calendar for July 2015. The program first calcuates number of days that have elapsed from 01/01/01 upto 30/06/2015 and stores it in **tdays**. Then it finds out how many of these days could not be evened out into weeks by taking a % by 7. If the value stored in **fday** is 0, it means that all days got evened out, hence coming day, i.e. 01/07/2015 is beginning of a fresh week, i.e. Monday. If **fday** is 1 then coming day is Tuesday, if it is 2 then coming day is Wednesday, etc.

Once the day is determined, the column below which the calendar has to start gets decided and this is recorded in **c**. Then the printing takes place—firstly the name of month and year, then Mon, Tue, etc. and finally the dates through a **for** loop.

Note that the month is printed by picking the appropriate value from **months[ ]** array, whereas the dates are printed in suitable row and column by appropriately updating the values of **r** and **c**.

Before printing is started, the screen is cleared by calling the **system( )** function. Before printing each date the cursor is suitably positioned on the screen by calling the **gotoxy( )** function. In the **gotoxy( )** function we have printed the ANSI escape code using:

printf ( "%c[%d;%df", 0x1B, y, x ) ;

The ANSI escape codes (or escape sequences) are a method using in-band signaling to control the formatting, color, and other output options on video text terminals. To encode this formatting information, certain sequences of bytes are embedded into the text, which the terminal looks for and interprets as commands, rather than as character codes. 0x1B is decimal 27 which is the ASCII value of Esc. The sequence 27[10;20 when sent to terminal window would position the cursor at 10th row, 20th column.

In NetBeans one more setting needs to be done to display the output in suitable row and column. Right click on the project name in the "Projects" window. Then select Properties -> select Run -> Change console type from internal terminal to external terminal. A black window would appear as an external terminal. All outuput of the program would be now sent to this external terminal window.

## Challenge 83

Write a program to sort a set of names stored in an array in alphabetical order.

*Index it*

## Solution

*bubble sort used to sort more elements*

```c
/* Sort strings alphabetically */
# include <stdio.h>

int main( )
{
    char  *str[ ] = {
                        "Rajesh",
                        "Ashish",
                        "Milind",
                        "Pushkar",
                        "Akash"
                    };

    char *t ;
    int i, j ;

    for ( i = 0 ; i < 5 ; i++ )
```

```
    {
        for ( j = i + 1 ; j < 5 ; j++ )
        {
            if ( ( strcmp ( str[ i ], str[ j ] ) ) > 0 )
            {
                t = str[ i ] ;
                str[ i ] = str[ j ] ;
                str[ j ] = t ;
            }
        }
    }

    for ( i = 0 ; i < 5 ; i++ )
        printf ( "%s\n", str[ i ] ) ;

    return 0 ;
}
```

*Using Strcmp to Sort elements*

## Sample Run

Akash
Ashish
Milind
Pushkar
Rajesh

## Explanation

**str[ ]** stores address of each string. The bubble sort logic is implemented using two for loops. Whether alphabetic order of two strings pointed by **str[ i ]** and **str[ j ]** is correct or not is determined from the value returned by **strcmp( )**. If the order is incorrect then the addresses stored in **str[ i ]** and **str[ j ]** are interchanged.

## Challenge 84

*Index it*

Write a program to generate and print all possible combinations of the characters present in a given string.

## Solution

```c
#include <stdio.h>
#include <string.h>

void permute ( char*, int, int ) ;
void swap ( char*, char* ) ;

int main( )
{
    char  str[ ] = "JOKE" ;
    int  n ;

    n = strlen ( str ) ;
    permute ( str, 0, n - 1 ) ;

    return 0 ;
}

void permute ( char  *str, int  begin, int  end )
{
    int  i ;

    if ( begin == end )
    {
        printf ( "%s\n", str ) ;
        return ;
    }
    else
    {
        for ( i = begin ; i <= end ; i++ )
        {
            swap ( str + begin, str + i ) ;
            permute ( str, begin + 1, end ) ;
            swap ( str + begin, str + i ) ;
        }
    }
}

void swap ( char  *s, char  *t )
```

*Handwritten annotations:*

Algorithm Similar to challenge 21 can also be used.

End Index

Start Index

— base case

Variable/ Parameter begin

— Recursive

Two Pointers to a char

```
{
    char ch ;

    ch = *s ;
    *s = *t ;
    *t = ch ;
}
```

*create a temp variable to swap values* (handwritten annotation)

## Sample Run

```
JOKE
JOEK
JKOE
JKEO
JEKO
JEOK
OJKE
OJEK
OKJE
OKEJ
OEKJ
OEJK
KOJE
KOEJ
KJOE
KJEO
KEJO
KEOJ
EOKJ
EOJK
EKOJ
EKJO
EJKO
EJOK
```

## Explanation

In the **permute( )** function in the **for** loop starting from the first position, we place all the characters in the string at this position one by one, and call the **permute( )** function recursively on the remaining part of the string. Once done with that, we replace the character at the first position to what it was initially. The following figure demonstrates this for a string "ABC".

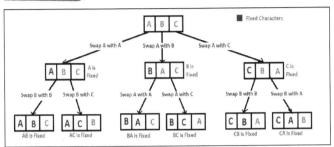

Figure 10.1. *All possible combination of 3 characters.*

## Challenge 85

Pending

Write a program that receives a 5-digit number and prints it out in large size as shown below:

5 char wide

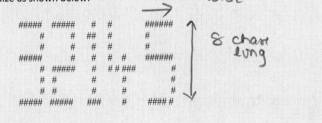

8 char long

Index it

## Solution

```
/* Display a given number in banner form */
#include <stdio.h>
#include <string.h>

void gotoxy ( int col, int row );

int main( )
{
```

```
int digits[ ][ 8 ][ 5 ] = {
                    {
                        1,1,1,1,1,
                        1,0,0,0,1,
                        1,0,0,0,1,
                        1,0,0,0,1,        O
                        1,0,0,0,1,
                        1,0,0,0,1,
                        1,0,0,0,1,
                        1,1,1,1,1
                    },
                    {
                        0,0,1,0,0,
                        0,1,1,0,0,
                        0,0,1,0,0,
                        0,0,1,0,0,        1
                        0,0,1,0,0,
                        0,0,1,0,0,
                        0,0,1,0,0,
                        0,1,1,1,0
                    },
                    {
                        1,1,1,1,1,
                        0,0,0,0,1,
                        0,0,0,0,1,
                        0,0,0,0,1,        2
                        1,1,1,1,1,
                        1,0,0,0,0,
                        1,0,0,0,0,
                        1,1,1,1,1
                    },
                    {
                        1,1,1,1,1,
                        0,0,0,0,1,
                        0,0,0,0,1,
                        1,1,1,1,1,
                        0,0,0,0,1,        3
                        0,0,0,0,1,
                        0,0,0,0,1,
                        1,1,1,1,1
                    },
```

```
{
    1,0,0,0,0,
    1,0,0,0,0,
    1,0,0,0,0,
    1,0,1,0,0,
    1,1,1,1,1,
    0,0,1,0,0,
    0,0,1,0,0,
    0,0,1,0,0
},
{
    1,1,1,1,1,
    1,0,0,0,0,
    1,0,0,0,0,
    1,1,1,1,1,
    0,0,0,0,1,
    0,0,0,0,1,
    0,0,0,0,1,
    1,1,1,1,1
},
{
    1,1,1,1,1,
    1,0,0,0,0,
    1,0,0,0,0,
    1,1,1,1,1,
    1,0,0,0,1,
    1,0,0,0,1,
    1,0,0,0,1,
    1,1,1,1,1
},
{
    1,1,1,1,1,
    0,0,0,0,1,
    0,0,0,0,1,
    0,0,0,0,1,
    0,0,0,0,1,
    0,0,0,0,1,
    0,0,0,0,1,
    0,0,0,0,1
},
{
```

4

5

6

7

```
                                    1,1,1,1,1,
                                    1,0,0,0,1,
                                    1,0,0,0,1,
                                    1,1,1,1,1,
                                    1,0,0,0,1,
                                    1,0,0,0,1,
                                    1,0,0,0,1,
                                    1,1,1,1,1
                        },
                        {
                                    1,1,1,1,1,
                                    1,0,0,0,1,
                                    1,0,0,0,1,
                                    1,1,1,1,1,
                                    0,0,0,0,1,
                                    0,0,0,0,1,
                                    0,0,0,0,1,
                                    1,1,1,1,1
                        }
                } ;
    char  str[ 6 ] ;
    int  i, j, k, l, r, c ;

    printf ( "\nEnter a 5 digit number: " ) ;
    scanf ( "%s", str ) ;

    if ( strlen ( str ) > 5 )
    {
        printf ( "Your number has more than 5 digits\n" ) ;
        return 1 ;
    }

    system ( "clear" ) ;
    i = 0 ;
    while ( str[ i ] != '\0' )
    {
        j = str[ i ] - 48 ;

        for ( r = 0, k = 0 ; r <= 7 ; k++, r++ )
        {
            for ( l = 0, c = i * 6 ; l <= 4 ; l++, c++ )
```

```
                {
                    if ( digits[ j ][ k ][ l ] == 1 )
                    {
                        gotoxy ( c, r ) ;
                        printf ( "#" ) ;
                    }
                }
            }
            i++ ;
        }
        printf ( "\n" ) ;

        return 0 ;
}

void gotoxy ( int  x, int  y )
{
    printf ( "%c[%d;%df", 0x1B, y, x ) ;
}
```

## Sample Run

```
#####   #  #      ######  #####
    #   ## #      #            #
    #   #  #      #            #
    #   #  #  #   ######  #####
#####   #  # # ###     #      #
#       #  #          #       #
#       #  #          #       #
#####  ###  #      #####  #####
```

## Explanation

Let us begin with the **digits[ ][ ][ ]** array. It is a collection of several 2D arrays, where each 2D array is a 8 row by 5 column matrix containing 0s and 1s. In this matrix where a digit is being drawn it contains a 1, whereas the empty space contains a 0. The number to be printed is received as a string, so while printing each character of the string is first converted into a digit by subtracting 48 (ASCII value of 0) from it.

Before printing, the screen is cleared by calling the **system( )** function. While printing through the **for** loops, firstly the appropriate matrix is picked up from the 3D array and then for all 1s present in this matrix # is printed, whereas all 0s are ignored. While printing 1s, the curosr is first suitably positioned on the screen using **gotoxy( )** function.

Don't forget to activate the external terminal window from Projects | Properties | Run | Console type.

For detailed explanation of **gotoxy( )** and external terminal window please refer explanation in Challenge 82.

## Challenge 86

Write a program that receives an integer (less than or equal to nine digits in length) and prints out the number in words. For example, if the number input is 12342, then the output should be Twelve Thousand Three Hundred Forty Two.

## Solution

```
/* Convert number to words */
#include<stdio.h>

void convert ( long, char [ ] ) ;

char *one[ ] = {                    → Skipped for zero
                " ", " One", " Two", " Three", " Four", " Five",
                " Six", " Seven", "Eight", " Nine", " Ten",
                " Eleven", " Twelve", " Thirteen", " Fourteen",
                "Fifteen", " Sixteen", " Seventeen", " Eighteen",
                " Nineteen"
            } ;

char *ten[ ] = {        ← Skipped for zero and one
                " ", " ", " Twenty", " Thirty", " Forty", " Fifty",
                " Sixty", " Seventy", " Eighty", " Ninety"
            } ;

int main( )
{
```

```
        long  num ;

        printf ( "\nEnter any Number (max 9 digits): " ) ;
        scanf ( "%ld", &num ) ;

        if ( num <= 0 )
            printf ( "No negative numbers please...\n" ) ;
        else
        {
            convert ( ( num / 10000000 ), "Crore" ) ;
            convert ( ( ( num / 100000 ) % 100 ), "Lakh" ) ;
            convert ( ( ( num / 1000 ) % 100 ), "Thousand" ) ;
            convert ( ( ( num / 100 ) % 10 ), "Hundred" ) ;
            convert ( ( num % 100 )," " ) ;
        }
}
```

```
void convert ( long n, char *s )
{
    if ( n > 19 )
        printf ( "%s %s ", ten[ n / 10 ], one[ n % 10 ] ) ;
    else
        printf ( "%s ", one[ n ] ) ;

    if ( n )
        printf ( "%s ", s ) ;
}
```

## Sample Run

Enter any Number (max 9 digits): 12345
Twelve Thousand Three Hundred Forty Five

## Explanation

The explanation of this program is skipped and the reader is encouraged
to execute the program and analyse its working on his own.

# 11 / Total Challenges: 5

## Structure Challenges

In real life we usually deal with entities that are collections of things, each thing having its own attributes, just as the entity we call a 'book' is a collection of things, such as title, author, call number, publisher, number of pages, date of publication, etc. As you can see, all this data is dissimilar—author is a string, whereas number of pages is an integer. For dealing with such collections, C provides a data type called 'structure'. A structure gathers together, different atoms of information that comprise a given entity. This chapter presents challenges related with structures.

## Challenge 87

Write a program to sort birth dates of employees stored in an array of structures.

## Solution

```
/* Sort as per birth dates */
#include <stdio.h>
#define MAX 5

struct employee          Struct tag
{
    char  emp_name[ 20 ] ;
    int  date ;
    int  month ;
    int  year ;
} ;

void sortdates ( struct employee*, int ) ;
void printemployees ( struct employee*, int ) ;
int compare ( struct employee, struct employee ) ;

int main( )
{
    struct employee e[ MAX ] = {
                                { "Rahul", 19, 11, 1992 },
                                { "Sameer", 24, 6, 1991 },
                                { "Prashant", 22, 11, 1993 },
                                { "Soujanya", 12, 12, 1992 },
                                { "Sarmishta", 14, 10, 1992 }
                              } ;

    sortdates ( e, MAX ) ;
    printemployees ( e, MAX ) ;
}

void sortdates ( struct employee *e, int  size )
{
```

*[handwritten: Index it]*

*[handwritten: Sort date using the compare function]*

```
    int  i, j ;

    for ( i = 0 ; i < size ; i++ )
    {
        for ( j = i + 1 ; j < size ; j++ )
        {
            if ( compare ( e[ i ], e[ j ] ) == 1 )
            {
                struct employee t = e[ i ] ;
                e[ i ] = e[ j ] ;
                e[ j ] = t ;
            }
        }
    }
}
```

*If the employee is older*

```
/* Returns 1 if first employee is older than the second */
int compare ( struct employee e1, struct employee e2 )
{
    if ( e1.year < e2.year )
        return 1 ;
    else if ( e1.year > e2.year )
        return 0 ;
    else
    {
        if ( e1.month < e2.month )
            return 1 ;
        else if ( e1.month > e2.month )
            return 0 ;
        else
        {
            if ( e1.date < e2.date )
                return 1 ;
            else if ( e2.date > e1.date )
                return 0 ;
            else
                return 0 ;
        }
    }
}
```

*— e1 is older than e2*

*— e1 is younger than e2*

*If they are born in the same year*

```
void printemployees ( struct employee* e, int size )
{
    int i ;

    for ( i = 0 ; i < size ; i++ )
        printf ( "%s %d.%d.%d\n", e[ i ].emp_name,
                e[ i ].date, e[ i ].month, e[ i ].year ) ;
}
```

*Pointer to a struct* (handwritten annotation)

## Sample Run

Prashant 22.11.1993
Soujanya 12.12.1992
Rahul 19.11.1992
Sarmishta 14.10.1992
Sameer 24.6.1991

## Explanation

The program uses the simple Bubble Sort logic to sort dates. In this logic, during the first iteration, first date is compared with all other dates. The positions of dates are exchanged in such a manner that the record with most recent date comes in the first position. This record is left undisturbed during rest of the iterations. During the second iteration, second date is compared with rest of the dates and the record with most recent date out of them is brought to second position. Similar procedure is followed during rest of the iterations.

The **compare( )** function is used to decide which out of the two dates is more recent by comparing the years, months and dates in that order.

## Challenge 88

Write a progam to implement a Linked List data structure.

## Solution

```
#include <stdio.h>
#include <malloc.h>
```

```
/* structure containing a data part and link part */
struct node           Struct tag
{
    int data ;
    struct node* link ;        ↘    Pointer  to  a  struct
};

void append ( struct node **, int ) ;
void addatbeg ( struct node **, int ) ;
void addafter ( struct node *, int, int ) ;
void display ( struct node * ) ;
int count ( struct node * ) ;
void del ( struct node **, int ) ;

int main( )
{
    struct node *p ;
    p = NULL ; /* empty linked list */

    printf ( "No. of elements in the Linked List = %d\n", count ( p ) ) ;
    append ( &p, 14 ) ;
    append ( &p, 30 ) ;
    append ( &p, 25 ) ;
    append ( &p, 42 ) ;
    append ( &p, 17 ) ;

    display ( p ) ;

    addatbeg ( &p, 999 ) ;
    addatbeg ( &p, 888 ) ;
    addatbeg ( &p, 777 ) ;

    display ( p ) ;

    addafter ( p, 7, 0 ) ;
    addafter ( p, 2, 1 ) ;
    addafter ( p, 5, 99 ) ;

    display ( p ) ;
    printf ( "No. of elements in the Linked List = %d\n", count ( p ) ) ;
```

```
        del ( &p, 99 ) ;
        del ( &p, 1 ) ;
        del ( &p, 10 ) ;

        display ( p ) ;
        printf ( "No. of elements in the linked list = %d\n", count ( p ) ) ;
        return 0 ;
}

/* adds a node at the end of a linked list */
void append ( struct node **q, int num )
{
        struct node *temp, *r ;

        if ( *q == NULL ) /* if the list is empty, create first node */
        {
            temp = ( struct node * ) malloc ( sizeof ( struct node ) ) ;
            temp -> data = num ;
            temp -> link = NULL ;
            *q = temp ;
        }
        else
        {
            temp = *q ;

            /* go to last node */
            while ( temp -> link != NULL )
                temp = temp -> link ;

            /* add node at the end */
            r = ( struct node * ) malloc ( sizeof ( struct node ) ) ;
            r -> data = num ;
            r -> link = NULL ;
            temp -> link = r ;
        }
}

/* adds a new node at the beginning of the linked list */
void addatbeg ( struct node **q, int num )
{
```

```
    struct node *temp ;

    /* add new node */
    temp = ( struct node * ) malloc ( sizeof ( struct node ) ) ;

    temp -> data = num ;
    temp -> link = *q ;
    *q = temp ;
}

/* adds a new node after the specified number of nodes */
void addafter ( struct node *q, int loc, int num )
{
    struct node *temp, *r ;
    int i ;

    if ( loc <= 0 )
    {
        printf ( "Invalid value for location. Unable to add element\n" ) ;
        return ;
    }

    temp = q ;
    /* skip to desired portion */
    for ( i = 0 ; i < loc ; i++ )
    {
        temp = temp -> link ;

        /* if end of linked list is encountered */
        if ( temp == NULL )
        {
            printf ( "There are less than %d elements in list\n", loc ) ;
            return ;
        }
    }

    /* insert new node */
    r = ( struct node * ) malloc ( sizeof ( struct node ) ) ;
    r -> data = num ;
    r -> link = temp -> link ;
    temp -> link = r ;
```

```
}

/* displays the contents of the linked list */
void display ( struct node *q )
{
    /* traverse the entire linked list */
    while ( q != NULL )
    {
        printf ( "%d ", q -> data ) ;
        q = q -> link ;
    }
    printf ( "\n" ) ;
}

/* counts the number of nodes present in the linked list */
int count ( struct node * q )
{
    int c = 0 ;

    /* traverse the entire linked list */
    while ( q != NULL )
    {
        q = q -> link ;
        c++ ;
    }

    return c ;
}

/* deletes the specified node from the linked list */
void del ( struct node **q, int num )
{
    struct node *old, *temp ;

    temp = *q ;

    while ( temp != NULL )
    {
        if ( temp -> data == num )
        {
            /* if node to be deleted is the first node in the linked list */
```

```
            if ( temp == *q )
                *q = temp -> link ;
            else
                old -> link = temp -> link ;

            /* free the memory occupied by the node */
            free ( temp ) ;
            return ;
        }
        else
        {
            old = temp ;
            temp = temp -> link ;
        }
    }

    printf ( "Element %d not found in Linked List\n", num ) ;
}
```

## Sample Run

```
Number of elements in the linked list = 0
14 30 25 42 17
777 888 999 14 30 25 42 17
777 99 1 0 888 999 14 30 25 42 17
Number of elements in the linked list = 11
Element 10 is not present in the linked list.
777 0 888 999 14 30 25 42 17
Number of elements in the linked list = 9
```

## Explanation

While the elements of an array occupy contiguous memory locations, those of a linked list are not constrained to be stored in adjacent locations. The individual elements are stored "somewhere" in memory, rather like a family dispersed, but still bound together. The order of the elements is maintained by explicit links between them. For instance, the marks obtained by different students can be stored in a linked list as shown in Figure 11.1.

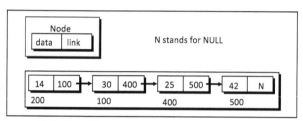

Figure 11.1. *Linked list.*

Observe that the linked list is a collection of elements called nodes, each of which stores two items of information—an element of the list and a link. A link is a pointer or an address that indicates explicitly the location of the node containing the successor of the list element. In Figure 11.1, the arrows represent the links. The **data** part of each node consists of the marks obtained by a student and the **link** part is a pointer to the next node. The **NULL** in the last node indicates that this is the last node in the list.

There are several operations that we can think of performing on linked lists. Our program shows how to build a linked list by adding new nodes at the beginning, at the end or in the middle of the linked list. It also contains a function **display( )** which displays all the nodes present in the linked list and a function **del( )** which can delete any node in the linked list.

To begin with we have defined a structure for a node. It contains a data part and a link part. The variable **p** has been declared as pointer to a node. We have used this pointer as pointer to the first node in the linked list. No matter how many nodes get added to the linked list, **p** would continue to pointer to the first node in the list. When no node has been added to the list, **p** has been set to **NULL** to indicate that the list is empty.

The **append( )** function has to deal with two situations:

(a)  The node is being added to an empty list.
(b)  The node is being added at the end of an existing list.

In the first case, the condition

if ( *q == NULL )

gets satisfied. Hence, space is allocated for the node using **malloc( )**. Data and the link part of this node are set up using the statements

```
temp -> data = num ;
temp -> link = NULL ;
```

Lastly, **p** is made to point to this node, since the first node has been added to the list and **p** must always point to the first node. Note that **\*q** is nothing but equal to **p**.

In the other case, when the linked list is not empty, the condition

```
if ( *q == NULL )
```

would fail, since **\*q** (i.e. **p** is non-**NULL**). Now **temp** is made to point to the first node in the list through the statement

```
temp = *q ;
```

Then using **temp** we have traversed through the entire linked list using the statements

```
while ( temp -> link != NULL )
    temp = temp -> link ;
```

The position of the pointers before and after traversing the linked list is shown in Figure 11.2.

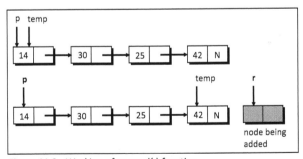

Figure 11.2. *Working of append( ) function.*

Each time through the loop the statement **temp = temp -> link** makes **temp** point to the next node in the list. When **temp** reaches the last node the condition **temp -> link != NULL** would fail. Once outside the loop we allocate space for the new node through the statement r = ( struct node * ) malloc ( sizeof ( struct node ) ) ;

Once the space has been allocated for the new node its **data** part is stuffed with **num** and the **link** part with **NULL**. Note that this node is now going to be the last Node in the list.

All that now remains to be done is connecting the previous last node with the new last node. The previous last node is being pointed to by **temp** and the new last node is being pointed to by **r**. They are connected through the statement

temp -> link = r ;

this link gets established.

There is often a confusion as to how the statement **temp = temp -> link** makes **temp** point to the next node in the list. Let us understand this with the help of an example. Suppose in a linked list containing 4 nodes, **temp** is pointing at the first node. This is shown in Figure 11.3.

Figure 11.3. *Connection of nodes.*

Instead of showing the links to the next node we have shown the addresses of the next node in the link part of each node.

When we execute the statement

temp = temp -> link ;

the right hand side yields **100**. This address is now stored in **temp**. As a result, **temp** starts pointing to the node present at address **100**. In effect the statement has shifted **temp** so that it has started pointing to the next node in the list.

Let us now understand the **addatbeg( )** function. Suppose there are already 5 nodes in the list and we wish to add a new node at the beginning of this existing linked list. This situation is shown in Figure 11.4.

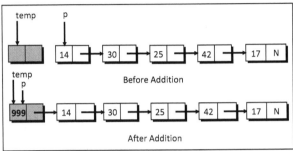

Figure 11.4. *Working of addatbeg( ) function.*

For adding a new node at the beginning, firstly space is allocated for this node and data is stored in it through the statement

temp -> data = num ;

Now we need to make the **link** part of this node point to the existing first node. This has been achieved through the statement

temp -> link = *q ;

Lastly, this new node must be made the first node in the list. This has been attained through the statement

*q = temp ;

The **addafter( )** function permits us to add a new node after a specified number of node in the linked list.

To begin with, through a loop we skip the desired number of nodes after which a new node is to be added. Suppose we wish to add a new node containing data as **99** after the 3$^{rd}$ node in the list. The position of pointers once the control reaches outside the **for** loop is shown in Figure 11.5. Now space is allocated for the node to be inserted and **99** is stored in the data part of it.

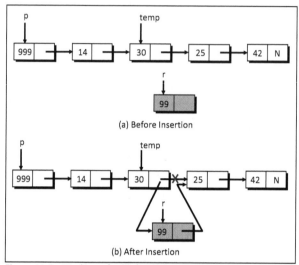

Figure 11.5. Working of *addafter( )* function.

All that remains to be done is readjustment of links such that **99** goes in between **30** and **25**. This is achieved through the statements

r -> link = temp -> link ;
temp -> link = r ;

The first statement makes link part of node containing **99** to point to the node containing **25**. The second statement ensures that the link part of node containing **30** points to the node containing **99**. On execution of the second statement the earlier link between **30** and **25** is severed. So now **30** no longer points to **25**, it points to **99**.

The **display( )** and **count( )** functions are straight forward. I leave them for you to understand.

That brings us to the last function in the program i.e. **del( )**. In this function through the **while** loop, we have traversed through the entire linked list, checking at each node, whether it is the node to be deleted. If so, we have checked if the node being deleted is the first node in the linked list. If it is so, we have simply shifted **p** (which is same as **\*q**) to the next node and then deleted the earlier node.

If the node to be deleted is an intermediate node, then the position of various pointers and links before and after the deletion is shown in Figure 11.6.

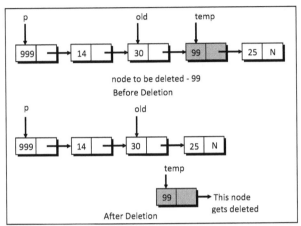

Figure 11.6. *Working of* ***del( )*** *function.*

## Challenge 89

Write a program to implement stack data structure as a linked list.

## Solution

```
/* Implementation of stack as a linked list */
#include <stdio.h>
#include <stdlib.h>

#define TRUE 1
#define FALSE 0

struct node
{
    int data ;
    struct node *link ;
```

```
} ;

void push ( struct node**, int ) ;
int pop ( struct node** ) ;
void delstack ( struct node** ) ;

int  empty = TRUE ;

int main ( )
{
    struct node *s = NULL ;
    int  i ;

    push ( &s, 14 ) ;
    push ( &s, -3 ) ;
    push ( &s, 18 ) ;
    push ( &s, 29 ) ;
    push ( &s, 31 ) ;
    push ( &s, 56 ) ;
    push ( &s, 14 ) ;

    i = pop ( &s ) ;
    if ( empty == FALSE )
        printf ( "Item popped = %d\n", i ) ;

    i = pop ( &s ) ;
    if ( empty == FALSE )
        printf ( "Item popped = %d\n", i ) ;

    i = pop ( &s ) ;
    if ( empty == FALSE )
        printf ( "Item popped = %d\n", i ) ;

    delstack ( &s ) ;

    return 0 ;
}

void push ( struct node **top, int  n )
{
    struct node *temp ;
```

```
    temp = ( struct node* ) malloc ( sizeof ( struct node ) ) ;

    if ( temp == NULL )
    {
        printf ( "Stack is full\n" ) ;
        return ;
    }

    temp -> data = n ;
    temp -> link = *top ;
    *top = temp ;
    empty = FALSE ;
}

int pop ( struct node **top )
{
    struct node *temp ;
    int  data ;

    if ( *top == NULL )
    {
        printf ( "Stack is empty\n" ) ;
        empty = TRUE ;
        return -1 ;
    }

    temp = *top ;
    data = temp -> data ;
    *top = temp -> link ;

    free ( temp ) ;

    return data ;
}

void delstack ( struct node **top )
{
    struct node *temp ;

    if ( *top == NULL )
```

```
        return ;

    while ( *top != NULL )
    {
        temp = *top ;
        *top = temp -> link ;
        free ( temp ) ;
    }
}
```

## Sample Run

Item popped: 16
Item popped: 31
Item popped: 29

## Explanation

The stack as linked list is represented as a singly connected list. Each node in the linked list contains the data and a pointer that gives location of the next node in the list. The pointer to the beginning of the list serves the purpose of the top of the stack. Figure 11.7 shows the linked list representation of a stack.

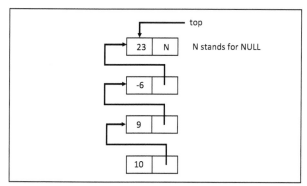

Figure 11.7. *Representation of stack as a linked list.*

Let us now see a program that implements stack as a linked list.

Here we have designed a structure called **node**. The variable **s** is a pointer to the structure **node**. Initially **s** is set to **NULL** to indicate that the stack is empty. In every call to the function **push( )** we are creating a new node dynamically. As long as there is enough space for dynamic memory allocation **temp** would never become **NULL**. If value of **temp** happens to be **NULL** then that would be the stage when stack would become full.

After, creating a new node, the pointer **s** should point to the newly created item of the list. Hence we have assigned the address of this new node to **s** using the pointer **top**. The stack as a linked list would grow as shown in Figure 11.8. Once an element is pushed to the stack we are setting a global variable **empty** to FALSE.

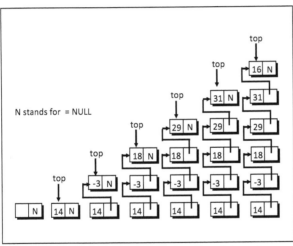

Figure 11.8. *Stack as a linked list after insertion of elements.*

In the **pop( )** function, first we are checking whether or not a stack is empty. If the stack is empty then a message 'Stack is empty.' gets displayed. If the stack is not empty then the topmost item gets removed from the list. The stack after removing three items from the list would be as shown in Figure 11.9.

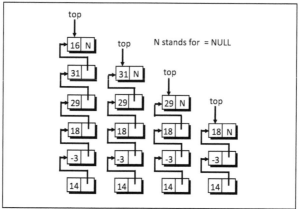

Figure 11.9. *Stack as a linked list after deletion of elements.*

## Challenge 90

Write a program to implement Queue data structure as a linked list.

## Solution

```
/* Implementation of queue as a linked list */
#include <stdio.h>
#include <stdlib.h>

#define TRUE 1
#define FALSE 0

struct node
{
    int  data ;
    struct node *link ;
} ;

struct queue
{
```

```
    struct node *front ;
    struct node *rear ;
} ;

int  empty ;

void initqueue ( struct queue* ) ;
void add ( struct queue*, int ) ;
int delete ( struct queue* ) ;
void delqueue ( struct queue* ) ;

int main ( )
{
    struct queue  a ;
    int  i ;

    initqueue ( &a ) ;

    add ( &a, 11 ) ;
    add ( &a, -8 ) ;
    add ( &a, 23 ) ;
    add ( &a, 19 ) ;
    add ( &a, 15 ) ;
    add ( &a, 16 ) ;
    add ( &a, 28 ) ;

    i = delete ( &a ) ;
    if ( empty == FALSE )
        printf ( "Element removed from the queue = %d\n", i ) ;

    i = delete ( &a ) ;
    if ( empty == FALSE )
        printf ( "Element removed from the queue = %d\n", i ) ;

    i = delete ( &a ) ;
    if ( empty == FALSE )
        printf ( "Element removed from the queue = %d\n", i ) ;

    delqueue ( &a ) ;
}
```

```
void initqueue ( struct queue *q )
{
    q -> front = NULL ;
    q -> rear = NULL ;
    empty = TRUE ;
}

void add ( struct queue *q, int  n )
{
    struct node *temp ;
    temp = ( struct node* ) malloc ( sizeof ( struct node ) ) ;

    if ( temp == NULL )
    {
        printf ( "Queue is full\n" ) ;
        return ;
    }

    temp -> data = n ;
    temp -> link = NULL ;

    if ( q -> front == NULL )
    {
        q -> front = temp ;
        q -> rear = temp ;
    }
    else
    {
        q -> rear -> link = temp ;
        q -> rear = temp ;
    }
    empty = FALSE ;
}

int delete ( struct queue *q )
{
    struct node *temp ;
    int  data ;

    if ( q -> front == NULL )
    {
```

```
        printf ( "Queue is empty\n" ) ;
        empty = TRUE ;
        return -1 ;
    }

    temp = q -> front ;
    data = temp -> data ;
    q -> front = temp -> link ;

    free ( temp ) ;

    return data ;
}

void delqueue ( struct queue *q )
{
    struct node *temp ;

    if ( q -> front == NULL )
        return ;

    while ( q -> front != NULL )
    {
        temp = q -> front ;
        q -> front = temp -> link ;
        free ( temp ) ;
    }
    q -> rear = NULL ;
}
```

## Sample Run

```
Element removed from the queue = 11
Element removed from the queue = -8
Element removed from the queue = 23
```

## Explanation

Queue can also be represented using a linked list. As discussed earlier, linked lists do not have any restrictions on the number of elements it can hold. Space for the elements in a linked list is allocated dynamically, hence it can grow as long as there is enough memory available for dynamic allocation. The item in the queue represented as a linked list would be a structure as shown below:

```
struct node
{
    <dataType> data ;
    struct node *link ;
};
```

where dataType represents the type of data such as an **int, float, char,** etc. Figure 11.10 shows the representation of a queue as a linked list.

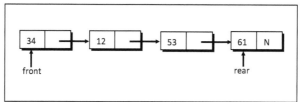

**Figure** 11.10. *Queue as a Linked List.*

In this program the structure **queue** contains two data members, **front** and **rear**, both are of the type pointers to the structure **node**. To begin with, the queue is empty hence both **front** and **rear** are set to **NULL.** Also the global variable **empty** is set to TRUE.

The **addq( )** function adds a new element at the rear end of the list. If the element added is the first element, then both **front** and **rear** are made to point to the new node. However, if the element added is not the first element then only **rear** is made to point to the new node, whereas **front** continues to point to the first node in the list. Each time an element is addes to the queue, **empty** is set to FALSE.

The **delq( )** function removes an element from the list which is at the front end of the list. Removal of an element from the list actually deletes the node to which **front** is pointing. After deletion of a node, **front** is made to point to the next node that comes in the list, whereas **rear** continues to point to the last node in the list.

The function **delqueue( )** is called before the function **main( )** comes to an end. This is done because the memory allocated for the existing nodes in the list must be de-allocated.

## Challenge 91

A record contains name of cricketer, his age, number of test matches that he has played and the average runs that he has scored in each test match. Create an array of structures to hold records of 20 such cricketers and then write a program to read these records and arrange them in ascending order by average runs. Use the **qsort( )** standard library function.

### Solution

```c
/* Create array of structures, sort and display */
# include <stdio.h>
# include <stdlib.h>

#define MAX 10
void fun( ) ;
int  comp_fun ( const void *, const void * ) ;
void sortbyavg( ) ;
void display( ) ;
void setdata( ) ;

struct cric_player
{
    char  name[ 20 ] ;
    int  age ;
    int  notest ;
    int  avgrun ;
} ;
struct cric_player cp[ MAX ] ;

int main( )
{
    /* set the values of the structure elements */
    setdata( ) ;
```

```
        /* sort the array of structures */
        sortbyavg( ) ;
        printf ( "Data sorted on Average Runs:\n" ) ;
        display( ) ;

        return 0 ;
}

/* Function to set the values of the structure */
void setdata( )
{
    int  i ;

    for ( i = 0 ; i < MAX ; i++ )
    {
        printf ( "Enter name, age, matches played, average:\n" ) ;
        fflush ( stdin ) ;
        scanf ( "%s %d %d %d", &cp[ i ].name, &cp[ i ].age,
                            &cp[ i ].notest, &cp[ i ].avgrun ) ;
    }
}

/* Function used for sorting the array of structures */
void sortbyavg( )
{
    struct cric_player t ;
    qsort ( ( struct cric_player * ) cp, MAX, sizeof ( cp[ 0 ] ), comp_fun ) ;
}

int  comp_fun ( const void *p1, const void *p2 )
{
    float avg1, avg2 ;

    avg1 = ( ( struct cric_player * ) p1 ) -> avgrun ;
    avg2 = ( ( struct cric_player * ) p2 ) -> avgrun ;

    return ( avg1 - avg2 ) ;
}

/* Function to display all the entries present in the structure */
```

```
void display( )
{
    int  i ;

    for ( i = 0 ; i < MAX ; i++ )
    printf ( "%s\t%d\t%d\t%d\n", cp[ i ].name, cp[ i ].age, cp[ i ].notest,
                                cp[ i ].avgrun ) ;
}
```

## Sample Run

```
Enter name, age, matches played, average:
Dinesh 24 10 75
Enter name, age, matches played, average:
Suresh 24 12 77
Enter name, age, matches played, average:
Sanjay 21 13 68
Enter name, age, matches played, average:
Vinod 23 10 80
Enter name, age, matches played, average:
Sameer 21 10 55
Enter name, age, matches played, average:
Prashant 22 10 45
Enter name, age, matches played, average:
Roshan 22 10 55
Enter name, age, matches played, average:
Rakesh 22 10 46
Enter name, age, matches played, average:
Shekhar 28 13 44
Enter name, age, matches played, average:
Shyam 21 10 40
Data sorted on Average Runs:
Shyam     21    10    40
Ram       28    13    44
Prash     22    10    45
Rakesh    22    10    46
Sameer    21    10    55
Roshan    22    10    55
Sanjay    21    13    68
Dinesh    24    10    75
Suresh    24    12    77
```

Vinod        23     10     80

## Explanation

Here sorting of records is done by calling the **qsort( )** library function as shown below:

qsort ( ( struct cric_player * ) cp, MAX, sizeof ( cp[ 0 ] ), comp_fun ) ;

Four paremeters are passed to **qsort( )**:
- Base address of the array being sorted
- Number of elements in the array
- Size of individual element of the array
- Base address of the comparison function

**qsort( )** calls the comparison function **comp_fun( )** using the address of the function passed to it. This means we can give any name to the comparison function.

The comparison function when called receives addresses of two elements that **qsort( )** is comparing at the moment. Since **qsort( )** is a generic function that can be used to sort any array, the comparison function receives the addresses as **void** pointers. Hence it is necessary to cast these pointers suitably. In our case, we have converted them into **struct** pointers. Then using the **struct** pointers we have accessed **avgrun** element present in the structures being compared.

J O K E —

J O E K —

J K O E —

J K E O —

J E K O —

J E O K —

# 12 / Total Challenges: 4

# File IO Challenges

Often it becomes necessary to store data in a file rather than just store it in memory or display it on screen. At such times, file IO operations need to be done. This chapter presents challenges related with this aspect of C programming.

YASHAVANT & ADITYA KANETKAR'S

101 Challenges

In C Programming

Solve 101 Challenges to hone C Programming skills
Practise them to be a mature C programmer

## Challenge 92

Write a program to read a file and display its contents along with line numbers before each line.

## Solution

```
/* Program to display a files contents along with line numbers */
# include <stdio.h>
#include <stdlib.h>

int main( )
{
    FILE *fp ;
    char ch ;
    char source[ 67 ] ;
    int count = 1 ;

    puts ( "Enter the file name : " ) ;
    scanf ( "%s", source ) ;

    fp = fopen ( source, "r" ) ;

    if ( fp == NULL )
    {
        puts ( "Unable to open the file\n" ) ;
        exit ( 1 ) ;
    }

    printf ( "Filename : %s", source ) ;

    printf ( "\nLine: %d\t", count ) ;
    while ( ( ch = getc( fp ) ) != EOF )
    {
        if ( ch == '\n' )
        {
            count++ ;
            printf ( "\nLine: %d\t", count ) ;
        }
```

```
        else
            printf ( "%c", ch ) ;
    }

    fclose ( fp ) ;
    return 0 ;
}
```

## Sample Run

```
Enter the file name :
main.c
Filename : main.c
Line: 1 /* Program to display a file with line numbers */
Line: 2 # include <stdio.h>
Line: 3 #include <stdlib.h>
Line: 4
Line: 5 int main( )
Line: 6 {
Line: 7     FILE *fp ;
Line: 8     char ch ;
Line: 9     char  source[ 67 ] ;
Line: 10       int  count = 1 ;
Line: 11
Line: 12       puts ( "Enter the file name : " ) ;
Line: 13       scanf ( "%s", source ) ;
Line: 14
Line: 15       fp = fopen ( source, "r" ) ;
Line: 16
Line: 17       if ( fp == NULL )
Line: 18       {
Line: 19           puts ( "Unable to open the file\n" ) ;
Line: 20           exit ( 1 ) ;
Line: 21       }
Line: 22
Line: 23       printf ( "Filename : %s", source ) ;
Line: 24
Line: 25       printf ( "\nLine: %d\t", count ) ;
Line: 26       while ( ( ch = getc( fp ) ) != EOF )
Line: 27       {
Line: 28           if ( ch == '\n' )
```

```
Line: 29                {
Line: 30                    count++ ;
Line: 31                    printf ( "\nLine: %d\t", count ) ;
Line: 32                }
Line: 33                else
Line: 34                    printf ( "%c", ch ) ;
Line: 35            }
Line: 36
Line: 37        fclose ( fp ) ;
Line: 38        return 0 ;
Line: 39    }
Line: 40
```

## Explanation

The program opens the file supplied to **scanf( )** for reading using the **fopen( )** function. In the sample run we have given the same file as the one in which the program is stored.

Once the file is opened, through a **for** loop using the **getc( )** function the file is read character by character. Each time we come across a '\n' we increment the **count** and print the line number in a fresh line.

## Challenge 93

Suppose a file contains student's records with each record containing name and age of a student. Write a program to read these records and display them in sorted order by name.

## Solution

/* Read records from a file and display them in alphabetical order by names. 'STUDENT.DAT' file is already created. Data has been written to it using the fwrite( ) function. */

```c
# include <stdio.h>
# include <string.h>

int main( )
```

```
{
    FILE *fp ;
    struct stud
    {
        char name[ 40 ] ;
        int age ;
    } ;
    struct stud s, stud[ 10 ], temp ;
    int n, i, j ;

    fp = fopen ( "STUDENT.DAT", "rb" ) ;
    if ( fp == NULL )
    {
        printf ( "Cannot open file\n" ) ;
        return 0 ;
    }

    n = 0 ;
    while ( fread ( &s, sizeof ( s ), 1, fp ) == 1 )
    {
        stud[ n ] = s ;
        n++ ;
    }

    fclose ( fp ) ;

    for ( i = 0 ; i < n - 1 ; i++ )
    {
        for ( j = i + 1 ; j < n ; j++ )
        {
            if ( strcmp ( stud[ i ].name, stud[ j ].name ) > 0 )
            {
                temp = stud[ i ] ;
                stud[ i ] = stud[ j ] ;
                stud[ j ] = temp ;
            }
        }
    }

    for ( i = 0 ; i < n ; i++ )
        printf ( "Name: %s , age: %d\n", stud[ i ].name, stud[ i ].age ) ;
```

```
        return 0 ;
}
```

## Sample Run

```
Akash     21
Akshay    24
Bishnu    23
Deepak    21
Sudha     22
Surabhi   23
```

## Explanation

The program opens the file "student.dat" and reads it record by record. Each record read is stored in the array **stud[ ]**. Once the reading of the file is over, the usual Bubble Sort logic is used to sort records in alphabetical order by name. **strcmp( )** function's return value is used to determine which name is smaller than the other in alphabetical order.

## Challenge 94

Write a program to encrypt/decrypt a file using a substitution cipher. In this cipher each character read from the source file is substituted by a corresponding predetermined character and this character is written to the target file.

For example, if character 'A' is read from the source file, and if we have decided that every 'A' is to be substituted by '!', then a '!' would be written to the target file in place of every 'A'. Similarly, every 'B' would be substituted by '5' and so on.

## Solution

```
/* Encrypt / Decrypt a file using substitution cipher */
/* encdec.c */
# include <stdio.h>
```

```
void encrypt( ) ;
void decrypt( ) ;

FILE  *fs, *ft ;

int main ( int  argc, char  *argv[ ] )
{
    if ( argc != 4 )
    {
        puts ( "Improper usage. Correct usage is:\n" ) ;
        puts ( "encdec <source filename> <target filename> E/D\n" ) ;
        exit ( 1 ) ;
    }

    fs = fopen ( argv[ 1 ], "r" ) ;
    if ( fs == NULL )
    {
        puts ( "Cannot open source file\n" ) ;
        exit ( 2 ) ;
    }

    ft = fopen ( argv[ 2 ], "w" ) ;
    if ( ft == NULL )
    {
        puts ( "Cannot open target file\n" ) ;
        fclose ( fs ) ;
        exit ( 3 ) ;
    }

    if ( *argv[ 3 ] == 'e' || *argv[ 3 ] == 'E' )
    {
        encrypt( ) ;
        printf ( "File %s encrypted successfully\n", argv[ 1 ] ) ;
    }
    else
    {
        if ( *argv[ 3 ] == 'd' || *argv[ 3 ] == 'D' )
        {
            decrypt( ) ;
            printf ( "File %s decrypted successfully\n", argv[ 1 ] ) ;
        }
```

```
        else
        {
            fclose ( fs ) ;
            fclose ( ft ) ;
            puts ( "Improper usage\n" ) ;
            exit ( 4 ) ;
        }
    }

    fclose ( fs ) ;
    fclose ( ft ) ;

    return 0 ;
}

void encrypt( )
{
    char  ch ;
    int  i ;
    char arr1[ 97 ] = "IOP{}asdfghjkl;'ASDFGHJKL:zxcvbn
                      m,./ZXCVBNM<>?`1234567890-=\~!@#
                      $%^&*( )_+|qwertyuiop[ ]QWERTYU" ;

    char arr2[ 97 ] = "`1234567890-=\~!@#$%^&*( )_+|qw
                      ertyuiop[ ]QWERTYUIOP{}asdfghjkl;'A
                      SDFGHJKL:zxcvbnm,./ZXCVBNM<>?" ;
    arr2[ 93 ] = '\\' ;
    arr1[ 93 ] = '\\' ;
    arr2[ 94 ] = '\"' ;
    arr1[ 94 ] = '\"' ;
    arr2[ 95 ] = '\n' ;
    arr1[ 95 ] = '\n' ;
    arr1[ 96 ] = '\t';
    arr2[ 96 ] = '\t' ;

    while ( ( ch = getc ( fs ) ) != EOF )
    {
        for ( i = 0 ; i <= 96 ; i++ )
        {
            if ( ch == arr1[ i ] )
```

```
                    break ;
            }
            putc ( arr2[ i ], ft ) ;
        }
    }

void decrypt( )
{
    char  ch ;
    int  i ;
    char  arr1[ 97 ] = " IOP{}asdfghjkl;'ASDFGHJKL:zxcvbn
                        m,./ZXCVBNM<>?`1234567890-=~!@#
                        $%^&*( )_+|qwertyuiop[  ]QWERTYU" ;
    char arr2[ 97 ] = " `1234567890-=~!@#$%^&*( )_+|qw
                        ertyuiop[  ]QWERTYUIOP{}asdfghjkl;'A
                        SDFGHJKL:zxcvbnm,./ZXCVBNM<>?" ;
    arr2[ 93 ] = '\\' ;
    arr1[ 93 ] = '\\' ;
    arr2[ 94 ] = '\"' ;
    arr1[ 94 ] = '\"' ;
    arr2[ 95 ] = '\n' ;
    arr1[ 95 ] = '\n' ;
    arr1[ 96 ] = '\t';
    arr2[ 96 ] = '\t' ;

    while ( ( ch = getc ( fs ) ) != EOF )
    {
        for ( i = 0 ; i <= 96 ; i++ )
        {
            if ( ch == arr2[ i ] )
                break ;
        }
        putc ( arr1[ i ], ft ) ;
    }
}
```

## Sample Runs

```
C:\> encdec  sample.c  newsample.c
Improper usage. Correct usage is:
encdec <source filename> <target filename> E/D
```

C:\> encdec sample.c newsample.c E
File sample.c encrypted successfully

C:\> encdec newsample.c sample.c D
File newsample.c decrypted successfully

## Explanation

The program first validates the input by checking whether 4 arguments have been provided or not, source and target files could be opened succesfully or not and the character E or D is provided as the last argument or not.

If the input is found to be valid then the substitution cipher is implemented through the **encrypt( )** and **decrypt( )** functions. These functions use two arrays **arr1[ ]** and **arr2[ ]** to store all characters that can be typed from the keyboard. Following care is taken while creating these arrays:

(a) Every character must occur only once in each array.

(b) Order of characters in the two arrays should be different.

(c) The same arrays must be used for encryption as well as decryption.

Note that the special characters like back slash, single quote, double quote, etc. are filled into the two arrays separately.

Once the arrays are created the encryption logic is simple. Each character read from the source file is searched in **arr1[ ]**. Once it is found, the corresponding character (i.e. the one present at $i^{th}$ position) from **arr2[ ]** is written to the target file.

The decryption logic works exactly opposite—search in **arr2[ ]** and replace from **arr1[ ]**.

## Challenge 95

Write a program "filecopy.c" that recevies source filename and target filename in the following format and then copies contents of the source file into target file using low level disk I/O functions:

filecopy <source filename> <target filename>

## Solution

```
/* File-copy program which copies text, .com and .exe files */
/* filecopy.c */

# include <fcntl.h>
# include <types.h>  /* if present in sys directory use "sys\\types.h" */
# include <stat.h>   /* if present in sys directory use "sys\\stat.h" */
# include <stdlib.h>
# include <stdio.h>

int main( int  argc, char *  argv[ ] )
{
    char  buffer[ 512 ] ;
    int  inhandle, outhandle, bytes ;

    if ( argc != 3 )
    {
        printf ( "Incorrect usage\n" ) ;
        printf ( "Correct usage: filecopy <spurce> <target>\n" ) ;
        exit ( 1 ) ;
    }

    inhandle = open ( argv[ 1 ], O_RDONLY | O_BINARY ) ;
    if ( inhandle == -1 )
    {
        printf ( "Cannot open source file" ) ;
        exit ( 2 ) ;
    }

    outhandle = open ( argv[ 2 ], O_CREAT | O_BINARY | O_WRONLY,
                      S_IWRITE ) ;
    if ( outhandle == -1 )
    {
        printf ( "Cannot open target file" ) ;
        close ( inhandle ) ;
        exit ( 3 ) ;
    }

    while ( 1 )
```

```
    {
        bytes = read ( inhandle, buffer, 512 ) ;

        if ( bytes > 0 )
            write ( outhandle, buffer, bytes ) ;
        else
            break ;
    }

    close ( inhandle ) ;
    close ( outhandle ) ;

    return 0 ;
}
```

## Sample Run

C:\> filecopy  pr1.c  newpr1.c

## Explanation

Instead of performing the I/O on a character-by-character basis this program reads a chunk of bytes from the source file and then writes this chunk into the target file. While doing so, the chunk would be read into the buffer and would be written to the file from the buffer. Hence to begin with we have created a character buffer called **buffer[ ]**. The size of this buffer is important for efficient operation. Depending on the operating system, buffers of certain sizes are handled more efficiently than others.

Next we have opened the source and target files using the **open( )** function. We have to supply to **open( )** the filename and the 'O-flags' to indicate the mode in which we want to open the file. These 'O-flags' are defined in the file "fcntl.h". So this file must be included in the program. When two or more O-flags are used together, they are combined using the bitwise OR operator ( | ). Note the second call to **open( )**.

outhandle = open ( target, O_CREAT | O_BINARY | O_WRONLY,
                   S_IWRITE ) ;

Since the target file doesn't exist when it is being opened, we have used the O_CREAT flag. Whenever O_CREAT flag is used, another argument must be added to **open( )** function to indicate the read/write status of the file to be created. This argument is called 'permission argument'. Permission arguments could be any of the following:

S_IWRITE    - Writing to the file permitted
S_IREAD     - Reading from the file permitted

To use these permissions, the files "types.h" and "stat.h" must be **#include**d in the program alongwith "fcntl.h".

Instead of returning a FILE pointer **open( )** returns an integer value called 'file handle'. This is a number assigned to a particular file, which is used thereafter to refer to the file. If **open( )** returns a value of -1, it means that the file couldn't be successfully opened.

The following statement reads the file or as much of it as will fit into the buffer:

bytes = read ( inhandle, buffer, 512 ) ;

The **read( )** function takes three arguments. The first argument is the file handle, the second is the address of the buffer and the third is the maximum number of bytes we want to read.

The **read( )** function returns the number of bytes actually read. This is an important number, since it may very well be less than the buffer size (512 bytes), and we will need to know just how full the buffer is before we can do anything with its contents. In our program we have assigned this number to the variable **bytes**.

For copying the file, we must use both the **read( )** and the **write( )** functions in a **while** loop. The **read( )** function returns the number of bytes actually read. This is assigned to the variable **bytes**. This value will be equal to the buffer size (512 bytes) until the end of file, when the buffer may only be partially full. The variable **bytes** therefore is used to tell **write( )**, as to how many bytes to write from the buffer to the target file.

# 13 / Total Challenges: 2

# Bitwise Operation Challenges

Programming languages are byte-oriented, whereas hardware tends to be bit-oriented. Bitwise operators allow us to delve inside the byte and see how it is constructed and how it can be manipulated effectively. This chapter offers challenges related to this.

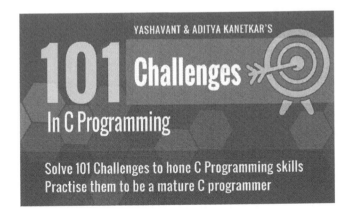

231

## Challenge 96

Define a **showbits( )** function that would print the binary value stored in a one-byte entity. Call it a couple of times to display binary contents of different values.

## Solution

```c
# include <stdio.h>
void showbits ( unsigned char ) ;

int main( )
{
    char  num1 = 15 ;
    char  num2 = 23 ;

    printf ( "\nDecimal %d is same as binary ", num1 ) ;
    showbits ( num1 ) ;

    printf ( "\nDecimal %d is same as binary ", num2 ) ;
    showbits ( num2 ) ;

    return 0 ;
}

void showbits ( unsigned char  n )
{
    int  i ;
    unsigned char  j, k, andmask ;

    for ( i = 7 ; i >= 0 ; i-- )
    {
        j = i ;
        andmask = 1 << j ;
        k = n & andmask ;
        k == 0 ? printf ( "0" ) : printf ( "1" ) ;
    }
}
```

## Sample Run

Decimal 15 is same as binary 00001111
Decimal 23 is same as binary 00010111

## Explanation

All that is being done in the **showbits( )** function is, using an AND operator and a variable **andmask**, we are checking the status of individual bits of **n**. If the bit is OFF we print a 0, otherwise we print a 1.

First time through the loop, the variable **andmask** will contain the value 10000000, which is obtained by left-shifting 1, seven places. If the variable **n's** most significant bit (leftmost bit) is 0, then **k** would contain a value 0, otherwise it would contain a non-zero value. If **k** contains 0, then **printf( )** will print out 0, otherwise it will print out 1.

In the second go-around of the loop, the value of **i** is decremented and hence the value of **andmask** changes, which will now be 01000000. This checks whether the next most significant bit is 1 or 0, and prints it out accordingly. The same operation is repeated for all bits in the number.

## Challenge 97

An animal could be a canine (dog, wolf, fox, etc.), a feline (cat, lynx, jaguar, etc.), a cetacean (whale, narwhal, etc.) or a marsupial (koala, wombat, etc.). The information whether a particular animal is canine, feline, cetacean, or marsupial is stored in bit number 0, 1, 2 and 3 respectively of a integer variable called **type**. Bit number 4 of the variable **type** stores the information about whether the animal is Carnivore or Herbivore.

For the following animal, complete the program to determine whether the animal is a herbivore or a carnivore. Also determine whether the animal is a canine, feline, cetacean or a marsupial.

```
struct animal
{
    char  name[ 30 ] ;
    int  type ;
```

```
}
struct  animal  a = { "OCELOT", 18 } ;
```

## Solution

```c
/* Determine the type of animal */
# include <stdio.h>

int main( )
{
    struct  animal
    {
        char  name[ 30 ] ;
        int  type ;
    } ;
    struct animal  a = { "OCELOT", 18 } ;
    int  ani ;

    printf ( "Animal is:\n" ) ;
    ani = a.type ;
    if ( ( ani & 1 ) == 1 )
        printf ( "Canine\n" ) ;
    if ( ( ani & 2 ) == 2 )
        printf ( "Feline\n" ) ;
    if ( ( ani & 4 ) == 4 )
        printf ( "Catacean\n" ) ;
    if ( ( ani & 8 ) == 8 )
        printf ( "Marsupial\n" ) ;

    printf ( "Animal is also a:\n" ) ;
    if ( ( ani & 16 ) == 16 )
        printf ( "Carnivore\n" ) ;
    else
        printf ( "Herbivore\n" ) ;

    return 0 ;
}
```

## Sample Run

Animal is:
Feline
Animal is also a:
Carnivore

## Explanation

Using the & operator repeatedly it is checked whether the corresponding bit is 1 or 0. For example, using

if ( ( ani & 4 ) == 4 )

it is being checked whether bit number 2 is 1 or 0.

Once the status of the bit is determined appopriate messages are printed.

# 14 / Total Challenges: 4

# Miscellaneous Challenges

There are certain useful programming features that are of immense help in certain programming strategies. These include bit fields, function pointers, functions with variable number of arguments and unions. This chapter presents challenges related to these features of C programming.

YASHAVANT & ADITYA KANETKAR'S

# 101 Challenges

## In C Programming

Solve 101 Challenges to hone C Programming skills
Practise them to be a mature C programmer

## Challenge 98

Create an array of four function pointers. Each pointer should point to a different function. Each of these functions should receive two integers and return a float. Using a loop call each of these functions using the addresses present in the array.

## Solution

```
/* Create and use an array of function pointers */
# include <stdio.h>

float fun1 ( int, int ) ;
float fun2 ( int, int ) ;
float fun3 ( int, int ) ;
float fun4 ( int, int ) ;

float fun1 ( int  i, int  j )
{
    printf ( "In fun1 i = %d j = %d\n", i, j ) ;
    return ( float )( i + j ) ;
}

float fun2 ( int  i, int  j )
{
    printf ( "In fun2 i = %d j = %d\n", i, j ) ;
    return ( float )( i - j ) ;
}

float fun3 ( int  i, int  j )
{
    printf ( "In fun3 i = %d j = %d\n", i, j ) ;
    return ( float )( i * j ) ;
}

float fun4 ( int  i, int  j )
{
    printf ( "In fun4 i = %d j = %d\n", i, j ) ;
    return ( float )( i / j ) ;
```

```
}

int main( )
{
    float ( *ptr[ 4 ] ) ( int, int ) ;
    float  f ;
    int  i ;

    ptr [ 0 ] = fun1 ;
    ptr [ 1 ] = fun2 ;
    ptr [ 2 ] = fun3 ;
    ptr [ 3 ] = fun4 ;

    for ( i = 0 ; i <= 3 ; i++ )
    {
        f = ( *ptr [ i ] ) ( 100, i + 1 ) ;
        printf ( "%f\n", f ) ;
    }

    return 0 ;
}
```

## Sample Run

```
In fun1 i = 100 j = 1
101.000000
In fun2 i = 100 j = 2
98.000000
In fun3 i = 100 j = 3
300.000000
In fun4 i = 100 j = 4
25.000000
```

## Explanation

Functions **fun1( )**, **fun2( )**, **fun3( )** and **fun4( )** all receive an **int** and a **float**, perform some arithmetic operation on them and return the **float** result. The addresses of these functions are stored in the array of function pointers **ptr[ ]**. Note the definition of this array. Then in a **for** loop using the expression f = ( *ptr [ i ] ) ( 100, i + 1 ) ;

the function whose address is present at the i[th] location in the array is called. During each call 100 and the current value of **i** is passed to the function and the result reurned by it is collected in **f** and printed out.

## Challenge 99

Write a function that receives variable number of arguments, where the arguments are the coordinates of a point. Based on the number of arguments received, the function should display type of shape (like a point, line, triangle, etc.) that can be drawn.

## Solution

```
/* Function with variable number of arguments */
# include <stdio.h>
# include <stdarg.h>

void shape ( int, ... ) ;

int main( )
{
    shape ( 1, 5, 10 ) ;
    shape ( 2, 1, 1, 10, 1 ) ;
    shape ( 3, 15,10, 5, 25, 20, 25 ) ;

    return 0 ;
}

void shape ( int  tot_pt, ... )
{
    int  count, x, y ;
    va_list  ptr ;

    switch ( tot_pt )
    {
        case 1 :
            printf ( "Type of shape is point\n" ) ;
            break ;
```

```
        case 2 :
            printf ( "Type of shape is line\n" ) ;
            break ;

        case 3 :
            printf ( "Type of shape is triangle\n" ) ;
            break ;
    }

    va_start ( ptr, tot_pt ) ;

    for ( count = 1 ; count <= tot_pt ; count++ )
    {
        x = va_arg ( ptr, int ) ;
        y = va_arg ( ptr, int ) ;
        printf ( "x%d = %d, y%d = %d\n", count, x, count, y ) ;
    }
}
```

## Sample Run

```
Type of shape is point
x1 = 5, y1 = 10
Type of shape is line
x1 = 1, y1 = 1
x2 = 10, y2 = 1
Type of shape is triangle
x1 = 15, y1 = 10
x2 = 5, y2 = 25
x3 = 20, y3 = 25
```

## Explanation

Note how the **shape( )** function has been declared. The ellipses ( ... )
indicate that the number of arguments after the first argument would
be variable. Here we are making three calls to **shape( )**. For each call the
first argument is the number of pairs of coordinates that follow the first
argument.

The value of the first argument passed to **shape( )** is collected in the variable **tot_pt**. **shape( )** begins with a declaration of a pointer **ptr** of the type **va_list**. Observe the next statement carefully.

va_start ( ptr, tot_pt ) ;

This statement sets up **ptr** such that it points to the first variable argument in the list. If we are considering the first call to **shape( )**, **ptr** would now point to 5. The statement **x = va_arg ( ptr, int )** would assign the integer being pointed to by **ptr** to **x**. Thus 5 would be assigned to **x**, and **ptr** would now start pointing to the next argument, i.e.,10. This is assigned to **y** by using **va_arg** once more. The rest of the program is fairly straightforward. We just keep picking up successive numbers in the list and keep printing them, till all the arguments in the list have been scanned.

Note that the **va_start** and **va_arg** macros are declared in the header file "stdarg.h", which needs to be included to be able to use these macros.

## Challenge 100

Write a program, which stores information about a date in a structure containing three members—day, month and year. Using bit fields the day number should get stored in first 5 bits of day, the month number in 4 bits of month and year in 12 bits of year. Write a program to read date of joining of 10 employees and display them in ascending order of year.

## Solution

```
/* To store joining dates using bit fields */
# include <stdio.h>

int main( )
{
    struct date
    {
        unsigned day : 5 ;
        unsigned month : 4 ;
        unsigned year : 12 ;
    } ;
    struct date  dt[ 10 ], temp ;
```

```
int  i, j, d, m, y ;

printf ( "Enter joining dates (dd-mm-yyyy) of 10 employees\n" ) ;

for ( i = 0 ; i < 10 ; i++ )
{
    scanf ( "%d %d %d", &d, &m, &y ) ;

    if ( ( ( d < 1 ) || ( d > 31 ) ) ||
         ( ( m < 1 ) || ( m > 12 ) ) ||
         ( ( y < 1900 ) || ( y > 2004 ) ) )
    {
        printf ( "Invalid date, enter new date\n" ) ;
        i-- ;
        continue ;
    }

    dt[ i ].day = d ;
    dt[ i ].month = m ;
    dt[ i ].year = y ;
}

for ( i = 0 ; i < 9 ; i++ )
{
    for ( j = i + 1 ; j < 10 ; j++ )
    {
        if ( dt[ j ].year < dt[ i ].year )
        {
            temp = dt[ i ] ;
            dt[ i ] = dt[ j ] ;
            dt[ j ] = temp ;
        }
    }
}

printf ( "Sorted Joining dates:\n" ) ;
for ( i = 0 ; i < 10 ; i++ )
    printf ( "%d %d %d\n", dt[ i ].day, dt[ i ].month, dt[ i ].year ) ;

return 0 ;
}
```

## Sample Run

Enter joining dates (dd-mm-yyyy) of 10 employees
1 1 2010
2 2 2013
3 3 2011
4 4 2014
5 5 2013
6 6 2016
7 7 2014
8 8 2012
9 9 2011
10 10 2013
Sorted Joining dates:
1 1 2010
3 3 2011
9 9 2011
8 8 2012
2 2 2013
5 5 2013
10 10 2013
7 7 2014
4 4 2014
6 6 2016

## Explanation

The colon ( : ) in the above declaration of **struct date** tells the compiler that we are talking about bit fields and the number after it tells how many bits to allot for the field. The bit fields are accessed using the normal way of accessing structure elements using the . operator. Sorting of dates is done using the Bubble Sort logic.

## Challenge 101

Write a program to read and store information about insurance policy holder. The information contains details like gender, whether the holder is minor/major, policy name and duration of the policy. Make use of bit-fields to store this information.

## Solution

```
# include <stdio.h>
# include <string.h>

int main( )
{
    struct  policy_holder
    {
        unsigned  gender : 1 ;
        unsigned  status : 1 ;
        char  name[ 20 ] ;
        unsigned  dr : 5 ;
    } ;
    struct policy_holder  h ;
    int  g, s, d ;
    char  n[ 20 ] ;

    printf ( "Enter gender (0-Male, 1-Female):\n" ) ;
    scanf ( "%d", &g ) ;

    printf ( "Enter status (0-Minor, 1-Major):\n" ) ;
    scanf ( "%d", &s ) ;

    printf ( "Enter name of the policy holder:\n" ) ;
    scanf ( "%s", n ) ;

    printf ( "Enter duration (1 to 25 yrs) of the policy:\n" ) ;
    scanf ( "%d", &d ) ;

    h.gender = g ;
    h.status = s ;
```

```
        strcpy ( h.name, n ) ;
        h.dr = d ;

        printf ( "Name: %s\n", h.name ) ;
        printf ( "Gender: %s\n", h.gender == 0 ? "Male" : "Female" ) ;
        printf ( "Status: %s\n", h.status == 0 ? "Minor" : "Major" ) ;
        printf ( "Duration %d\n", h.dr ) ;

        return 0 ;
}
```

## Sample Run

Enter gender (0-Male, 1-Female):
0
Enter status (0-Minor, 1-Major):
1
Enter name of the policy holder:
Dinesh
Enter duration (1 to 25 yrs) of the policy:
10
Name: Dinesh
Gender: Male
Status: Major
Duration 10

## Explanation

Observe the structure declaration carefully. It uses bit fields. The :
(colon) in the declaration indicates tells the compiler how many bits to
allot for the field.

Once we have established a bit field, we can reference it just like any
other structure element, as shown in the following statements:

h.gender = g ;
h.status = s ;

Made in the USA
Middletown, DE
14 May 2020